How to Do *Everything* with

iTunes

for Macintosh and Windows

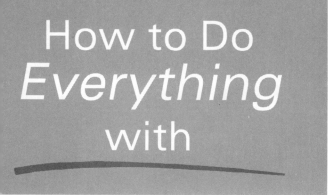

How to Do *Everything* with

iTunes
for Macintosh and Windows

Todd Stauffer

McGraw-Hill/Osborne

New York   Chicago   San Francisco   Lisbon
London   Madrid   Mexico City   Milan   New Delhi
San Juan   Seoul   Singapore   Sydney   Toronto

The McGraw·Hill Companies

McGraw-Hill/Osborne
2100 Powell Street, 10th Floor
Emeryville, California 94608
U.S.A.

To arrange bulk purchase discounts for sales promotions, premiums, or fund-raisers, please contact **McGraw-Hill**/Osborne at the above address. For information on translations or book distributors outside the U.S.A., please see the International Contact Information page immediately following the index of this book.

How to Do Everything with iTunes for Macintosh and Windows

1234567890 FGR FGR 019876543

ISBN 0-07-223196-3

Publisher:	Brandon A. Nordin
Vice President &	
Associate Publisher	Scott Rogers
Senior Acquisitions Editor	Jane Brownlow
Project Editor	Lisa Wolters-Broder
Acquisitions Coordinator	Athena Honore
Technical Editor	Clint Roberts
Copy Editor	Mike McGee
Proofreader	Susie Elkind
Indexer	Valerie Perry
Composition	Jean Butterfield, Tara A. Davis
Illustrators	Kathleen Edwards, Melinda Lytle
Series Design	Mickey Galicia

This book was composed with Corel VENTURA™ Publisher.

About the Author

Todd Stauffer is the author or co-author of more than 30 books about computing and the Internet, including *Get Creative: Digital Video Ideas* with Nina Parikh and *How to Do Everything with your iMac*, both from McGraw-Hill/Osborne. He's the originator of the How to Do Everything series. Todd is the publisher of the Jackson Free Press, a news and culture tabloid in Jackson, Miss., where he lives with Donna Ladd, his cat, her cat, and another cat that will have very little to do with the first two. He can be reached via his Web site at http://www.macblog.com/.

Contents at a Glance

Contents

Acknowledgments

I'd like to thank Jane Brownlow at McGraw-Hill/Osborne for the opportunity to write this book and for her help in getting the project off the ground. Also, special thanks to Lisa Wolters-Broder for patiently shepherding the process (which means waiting an extra day or so before prodding me for a new chapter) and helping to make things go as smoothly as one can possibly expect when I'm involved. Thanks also to Clint Roberts for technical editing and to Mike McGee for copy editing the book—without them... well, you don't want to know.

In addition, I'd like to thank Neil Salkind and the Studio B agency for their help on this project (and many others). Finally, I'd like to thank Donna Ladd for her constant support, as well as the staff of the Jackson Free Press for their forbearance when writing and editing took me away from the duties of my other day job.

Introduction

When Apple first announced iTunes, it seemed like a nice enough application—in fact, it did its job very well, integrating into Apple's package of "iApps" that include popular applications such as iMovie and iPhoto. iTunes did something else important—it came along as Apple was establishing a strategy in its hardware that meant including both FireWire and CD-RW (writeable CD) drives in many of its computer models.

iTunes made it possible to import songs from CDs and burn them to CD-R discs—fun, and handy for managing your collection of music, but a little limited. After all, you had to sit in front of your computer to access that music.

The iPod changed that. The iPod might not have been revolutionary, but it did two important things. First, it convinced everyday Mac users to carry a hard drive around with them in their pocket—something that's still pretty amazing, but is also what accounts for the iPod's enormous capacities. Second, it used iTunes as its interface, making the application that much more indispensable. And because your iPod can move with you (connecting, perhaps, to your car or home stereo) it gives you more of a reason to use your computer and iTunes for managing your digital audio files.

The iPod was so popular that it soon became clear that a Microsoft Windows version was necessary, which Apple released, offering MusicMatch software to work with the Windows iPod. But that wasn't good enough for Apple, particularly in light of the company's work to take iTunes in another important direction—the iTunes Music Store. Now iTunes for Mac users could buy digital music files and play those files back in iTunes and using an iPod—but Windows users couldn't until the fall of 2003.

At that point, iTunes for Mac and iTunes for Windows were released with nearly identical features and capabilities, a universal application for support of the iPod and the exact same access to the iTunes Music Store from both Macintosh (Mac OS X) and Windows (2000 and XP). On both platforms, iTunes is a sleek, brushed-metal application that's simple to get a handle on but that runs deep with features and complexity, as you'll see in *How to Do Everything with iTunes for Macintosh and Windows*.

Why This Book?

My goal with this book is to give you a comprehensive look at the tasks that are possible with iTunes for both Macintosh and Windows—not just the interface and menus, but how to really dig in and accomplish certain tasks with the application. Because the book is task-focused (as opposed to focused on the File menu, the Edit menu, etc.) you'll find that I very much want you to learn some of the fun and powerful things that iTunes can accomplish, such as how to:

- Create digital music files and translate between dominant file formats.

- Automatically organize your songs into playlists based on how large they are, how new they are, or how often you play them.

- Burn data CDs that can be used for backup, archiving, or moving your song collection to another computer.

- Buy songs, entire albums, or audiobooks from the iTunes Store and then play them back on the computers you use regularly.

- Dig into Web radio, streaming media, the iTunes visual effects, and what it takes to connect iTunes to your home stereo system.

- Learn the system behind iTunes—dealing with files, folder, file formats, translation, and creating audio files.

- Tweak, trick-out, and troubleshoot iTunes to truly make it work the way you want it to.

Whether you've had some experience with iTunes and want to dig deeper or you're just getting started with the whole digital music concept—perhaps you have an iPod in one hand and an iTunes CD-ROM in another—I think you'll find this text is enormously useful in uncovering some of the features and capabilities within iTunes.

How This Book is Organized

To move you from beginner to intermediate status, the text builds in complexity from the basics—how to start the application, play songs and import songs from

CDs (Chapter 1)—through the fundamentals of managing files (Chapter 2), burning CDs and DVDs of those songs (Chapter 3) to buying songs and managing those purchased songs (Chapter 4) from the iTunes Music Store. If you're already familiar with iTunes I think you'll still find these chapters worth skimming, particularly the Notes, Tips and How To sidebars that all tend to offer some interesting add-ons and tidbits.

Chapter 5 opens up the discussion, showing you a number of ways to customize iTunes both aurally and visually. Chapter 6 discusses the iPod and other digital music players, so if you have one of there or are considering such a purchase this chapter is worth checking out. Chapter 7 is for the power user—learn the keyboard commands for managing iTunes quickly, learn about customization and audio effects settings, and learn to share songs over a home or office network.

The remaining chapters are more advanced topics. Chapter 8 discusses the hierarchy of files and folders that happen behind the scenes with iTunes—if you need to more or restore a library of songs, or if you decide you want to store your songs in different places—this is an important chapter. Chapter 9 digs further into the digital audio files themselves with a look at MP3, AAC, and all the other three- and four-letter acronyms that make up the technology of digital audio. Chapter 9 not only discusses those technologies, but shows you how to use (or overcome) the differences for your iTunes-listening pleasure.

Chapter 10 divides things out a bit and offers a look at what's unique about the Mac vs. the Windows versions of iTunes—actually, their differences aren't that acute, but the technologies that they can work with in their respective operating systems is. On a Mac, iTunes can be controlled using AppleScript, for instance; in Windows, you'll find that Windows Media Audio is a dominant format that iTunes doesn't playback, so I've offered some explanations and pointers for using those technologies together.

Finally, Chapter 11 is a quick reference chapter for troubleshooting iTunes— if you're having trouble you can turn to that chapter for answers to frequently encountered issues or for pointers on where to find those answers. Appendix A offers a look at how to download and install iTunes if you don't already have it on your Mac or Windows PC. Appendix B talks about iTunes and America Online, and Appendix C discusses the iLife '04 suite of applications.

Aside from the chapter structure, you'll find that the book has some consistent elements throughout the text:

NOTE

A Note should reinforce something in the text or offer a mild caution— there are worth reading as they are generally something that I want to specifically call your attention to.

TIP *A Tip is something that you can worry about or not. Often a Tip is something that makes a task a bit easier or helps you think about it in a different way, although some Tips are just fun asides or "FYIs." In most cases ignoring Tips won't present a problem—but how much fun is that?*

You'll also see some special How To sidebars scattered throughout the book that are quick lessons on remarkable or important topics. In some cases you'll care to read them, in others you won't, but hopefully you'll find that they quickly get you up to speed on an interesting, if tangential, topic.

Contact Me

Have questions or comments? Think you may have found an error or are you confused about something in the text? I'll post a Web page to discuss this book, including links to the Web forum on my site and ways you can reach me directly to ask questions. Visit http://www.mac-upgrade.com/itunes/ to visit this book's Web page.

Thanks for your interest in *How to Do Everything with iTunes for Macintosh and Windows*, and here's to many hours of happy listening!

Chapter 1

Master the iTunes Basics

How to...

- Start up iTunes
- Understand the Interface
- Listen to CDs
- Rip Songs from CDs
- Set Encoding Options
- Import Digital Audio File

There's a lot to iTunes. While its primary function is as a digital music player application, it also enables you to manage a library of music, automate the playback of your favorite tunes, and accomplish other "killer" tasks such as burning audio CDs and loading and unloading songs from an external MP3 player.

In this first chapter, though, we're going to focus on the core competency of iTunes—getting songs onto your computer and playing them back. In most cases, you'll do this with your personal audio CDs—iTunes enables you to not only listen to your audio CDs, but you can take one of your CDs and import the songs from it, turning them into compressed digital music files that can be stored on your hard disk and played back any time. You'll also see how to get other types of audio files into iTunes, if you have them, and how to locate the digital music files that iTunes creates.

In the process, you'll be introduced to the iTunes interface and we'll discuss some of the audio formats that iTunes can work with and dig into some of the technological advances that have made what iTunes does possible.

Get Started with iTunes for Mac

Most Macs come with iTunes pre-installed, and more Windows machines today are coming this way as well—at least from certain manufacturers. If you have an iPod, an iTunes CD-ROM may have come with it, so you may have already installed the program. If this is the case, you can move right into launching iTunes for the first time and get started with the program, which we'll discuss here.

NOTE   *If you don't yet have iTunes, turn to Appendix A, where you can find information on downloading, installing, and updating iTunes for Macintosh and Windows.*

Launch iTunes on the Mac

To get started with iTunes on the Mac, you can launch its icon in the Dock by clicking it once or locating iTunes in the Applications folder and double-clicking to launch it. If this is the first time you've launched iTunes, you may see a legal agreement screen; click Accept to agree to the terms and then continue. This launches the iTunes Setup Assistant.

The Assistant walks you through the steps necessary to configure iTunes. Here's a quick look:

1. The first screen is a Welcome screen; click Next to continue.

2. On the Internet Audio screen, you can decide whether iTunes should be used for playing back Internet audio. (For instance, when you launch an audio stream in your web browser, do you want iTunes to launch and handle that audio?) You can also tell iTunes whether or not it's allowed to access the Internet automatically, or if it needs to ask you for permission to connect. (iTunes uses the Internet to find the names of CDs and song titles, to access web radio stations, and to access the iTunes Store.) Click Next when you've made your choices.

3. On the Find Music Files screen, you can choose whether or not you want iTunes to search your Mac for compatible audio files. Make your choice and click Next.

> NOTE   *Why wouldn't you want to search for music files? iTunes will automatically copy any found files from their current location to the Music folder in your home folder if they aren't already stored in your iTunes music folder. If you don't want those files copied (which could take up a lot of disk space if you have an extensive music library stored elsewhere), then choose No on the Find Music Files screen.*

4. On the iTunes Music Store screen, you get to choose whether or not the next step is to open the iTunes Music Store. Make your choice and click Next.

Now the iTunes interface will launch. First, iTunes will search for local music files if you've told it to. Then, it will display the iTunes window. If you chose to open the iTunes Music Store, you'll see it; if not, you'll see the main iTunes window.

Launch iTunes for Windows

Launching iTunes for Windows for the first time is actually pretty similar to launching iTunes on the Mac. Once you have it downloaded and installed (see Appendix A), the first time you launch the program you'll be greeted by the iTunes Setup Assistant. Here's how it works in Windows:

1. The first screen you'll see is the Welcome screen; click Next after you've read the text.

2. The next screen is the Find Music Files screen. If you select Yes, then iTunes will look in your My Music folder for MP3 and AAC digital audio files. Those that it finds, it will place in its library. You can also choose No (by clicking the radio button next to it) and iTunes will not search for music. Click Next to move to the next screen. On the Keep iTunes Music Folder Organized screen, iTunes is asking you if you want to allow iTunes to reorganize the folders and files that you already have stored in your My Music folder. If you already have an organization in that folder that's important to you, choose No; if you choose Yes, then iTunes will reorganize the folder so that songs are stored in folders by artist, which are then subdivided by album. (If you already have your music stored by genre or by some other system, then you probably don't want iTunes to change it.) Click Next once you've made your choice.

3. On the iTunes Music Screen, you'll choose whether you want to launch the iTunes Music Store when iTunes finishes launching itself or go to your iTunes Library (the main iTunes screen) instead. Make your choice and click Finish.

That's it. You're done with the Assistant. It will take a little time to look up songs in your My Music folder and then to query the CDDB database to get names and other information about those songs. From there, you'll be taken to the iTunes Music Store or your library, depending on the choices you made.

The Interface Basics

Once iTunes is launched, you're presented with its main interface window—if you end up finding iTunes useful on a regular basis, you'll get to know this window. Unlike some applications you may be familiar with, most of your interaction with iTunes will occur in this window. You'll occasionally open a dialog box and so on, but as far as managing and playing back songs, that happens mostly in the single iTunes window.

So, let's break it down a bit. The iTunes window is shown in Figure 1-1, along with callouts that point to its various features.

The following is a more detailed look at the different parts of that window:

■ **The source list**   On the left side of the window is the source list, where iTunes stores the various sources of audio you can play back. That includes the main library, where all of your digital audio files can be accessed and managed. (This consists of audio files that iTunes has automatically located, those that you've imported, and those that you've copied from your CD collection or bought from the iTunes Music Store.) You can also access the iTunes Music Store from the source list as well as from Internet radio stations. It's in the source list that you'll create your own playlists for managing your audio files.

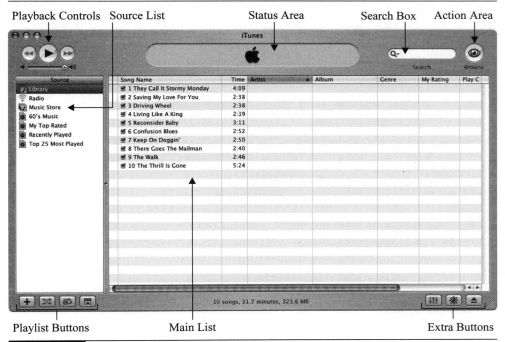

FIGURE 1-1   The main iTunes interface window

■ **The main list**   When you select one of the sources in the source list, a list of its songs (or stations or albums for purchase) will appear in the main list area. As you'll see in some depth in Chapter 2, the lists that you encounter can generally be sorted and searched in a variety of ways that make managing even a great number of songs relatively easy.

■ **Playback controls**   Up in the top-left corner are the controls used to play and pause songs, skip through them, or skip to the next (or previous) item in a list. They should look familiar if you've ever used a tape recorder, VCR, CD player, and so on. You've got a volume slider here, too.

■ **The status area**   Up at the top of the window, you'll get information about the song that's playing and the elapsed time. Just for fun, you can click the small arrow icon to change the status area to a visual representation of the song playing:

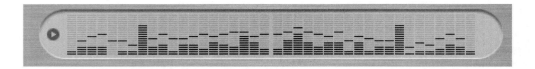

■ **The Search box**   The Search box enables you to quickly whittle down a list of songs in the main list.

■ **The Action button**   This button changes depending on what you're viewing in the main list.

■ **Playlist buttons**   The buttons in the lower-left corner enable you to create and manage playlists and other items in the source list. It's here, for instance, that you can set an audio CD or playlist to repeat or shuffle, as you might on a consumer CD player or the player in your car.

■ **Extra buttons**   On the lower-right side are buttons that enable you to access the built-in equalizer, the Visualizer (which displays patterns that are in sync with the music), and the Eject button for opening and closing your computer's CD/DVD drive.

And that's the interface. Now, let's move on to the very basics: playing songs.

Play Your Music

iTunes can play back a lot of different digital music. While focusing on digital music files (such as MP3s, which stand for MPEG Layer 3 audio files), in this section we'll cover playing songs that are in your library as well as playing songs from an audio CD. The two processes are simple and similar.

Play Songs

If you have a music file already in your iTunes Library—after the Setup Assistant has searched your home folder, for instance—you can play the song in one of two ways. The first is to simply double-click it in the main list. When you do, a small speaker icon will appear next to the song and you'll see information about that song displayed in the status area.

You should hear the song begin to play, and a small *scrubber bar* will appear in the status area. That bar can be used to quickly move to different parts of the song—just click and drag the small diamond back and forth. Note that you can also click the Elapsed Time entry to see other time information such as the Remaining Time and Total Time for the song.

The other way to play a song is to select it in the list and click the Play button in the playback controls at the top of the window, or press the spacebar. Again, this places the small speaker icon next to the song as it begins to play.

In either case, when you play a song, you've actually begun a process where iTunes will, by default, play every song in the current list after that song. (That's true as long as you don't have the Repeat One option enabled in the Controls menu. More on that in a moment.) So, if you're viewing your library and you play a song, all songs that come after it in the list will be played. When iTunes gets to the end of the list, it will stop playing. If you don't want a particular song in the list to play, click to remove the check mark next to that song's name in the list.

 *I say "lists" because the library isn't the only list that works this way. Playlists, which we'll cover in depth in Chapter 2, operate similarly. A playlist is just a subset of the songs in your library. When you view a playlist, you'll see a list of its songs in the main list area, and those songs will work according to these same rules.*

You can also get iTunes to play continuously, meaning that when it gets to the end of a list, it will loop back to the beginning. To turn on continuous playback, select Controls | Repeat All in the menu. (Choosing Controls | Repeat One will set iTunes to repeat the list once and then quit.) You can also click the Continue button in the lower-left corner of the interface to activate the Repeat All mode. Click it again to get into Repeat One mode.

You can also *shuffle* the songs in the active list. A shuffled list simply causes the songs to play in random order. To do this, choose Controls | Shuffle or click the Shuffle button in the lower-left corner.

To pause a song as it's playing, simply press the spacebar or click the Pause button (it's the same button as the Play button at the top left) and iTunes will pause. The Forward and Back buttons next to the Play/Pause button can be clicked once to go to the beginning of the song (for the left-facing arrows) or to the next song (the right-facing arrows). You can also click and hold on one of those arrow buttons to go forward or backward within the same song; when you release the mouse button, playback continues.

The volume slider enables you to click and drag along the slider to change the volume level. You can also use the ⌘ key (on a Mac) or the CTRL key (in Windows) and the keyboard up and down arrows to change volume levels. SHIFT-⌘-down arrow (SHIFT-CTRL-down arrow in Windows) will mute iTunes.

NOTE *iTunes has a volume control that's separate from your computer's main volume—when you change the setting in iTunes, you're only affecting iTunes and not the volume setting on your computer. If you want to set the main volume, you'll need to access that particular preference in Windows or the Mac OS X, depending on which one you're using. (In Windows, you can generally change the main volume via the speaker icon in the System Tray at the bottom-right of your display; in Mac OS X, you may have a volume menu icon in the top-right corner of your display.)*

Play a CD

Playing an audio CD is really very similar to playing songs out of your iTunes Library—the only major difference is that you'll select the CD in the source list before playing it.

To begin, place an audio CD in your Mac's CD or DVD drive. The CD can either be store-bought or one that's been created as an audio CD by computer software—in most cases, iTunes should not have much trouble with CDs that have been *burned* in other software. When the CD is *mounted* by your computer—that is, recognized and made available for use—iTunes will query the Gracenote CDDB database, which is an online service that automatically provides the names of albums and songs to computer programs that know how to access it. If your computer is set to automatically connect to the Internet, this query is made automatically; if not, you'll see generic entries for the CD and its songs.

▲	Song Name	Time	Artist
1	☑ Track 01	4:10	
2	☑ Track 02	3:41	
3	☑ Track 03	1:56	
4	☑ Track 04	2:53	
5	☑ Track 05	3:27	

Once the CD is recognized by iTunes and the CDDB database is queried, it will appear in the source list, as shown in Figure 1-2.

To play a song or audio track from the CD, simply double-click it, or select it and click the Play button or press the spacebar. From here, all of the controls are the same as discussed in the previous section "Play Songs"—you can use the Repeat command, the Shuffle command, and so on.

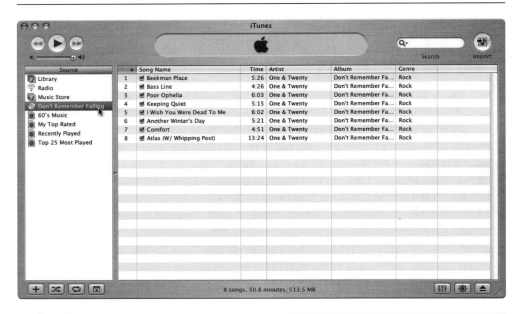

FIGURE 1-2 The CD appears in the source list after it's been recognized by iTunes.

You can rename a CD in the source list if you so desire. Click the CD to highlight it if it isn't already highlighted, then click again to highlight the name for editing. The name appears in reverse type with a box around it. Now, just type in the new name to change it.

Add Music to the Library

After familiarizing yourself with iTunes, you'll probably be chomping at the bit to start adding songs to your library. After all, iTunes is more than just an audio playback application—its strength really shines through when you're managing a fair number of music and audio files. To get to that point, though, you've got to get the music into iTunes.

You can do that in a couple of ways. In this section, we'll focus on *importing* songs from CDs, which is essentially translating tracks on a CD from their native file format into iTunes-compatible formats such as AAC or MP3. This creates a copy of the audio track as a separate file that's then stored on your Mac. In fact, you can transfer the song to your iPod or similar digital music device, and even relocate the file for use on different computers.

If you already have songs or audio files in digital audio format, you can import those into iTunes easily as well. We'll discuss that in this section, too. The other main way to get songs into iTunes—buying them from the iTunes Store—is something we'll save for Chapter 4.

CAUTION *I'll be mentioning this throughout the book: Don't steal music! You should work only with CDs and audio files which you either own the copyright to or have the right to duplicate. The best way to keep yourself out of trouble is to only import songs into iTunes from CDs that you own, and avoid giving digital music files to others.*

Import Songs from CDs

You probably already have some audio CDs that you'd like to add to your iTunes Library. To do that, you begin by popping the CD into your computer and waiting for it to mount in iTunes. When it's mounted, you're ready to import those songs into digital audio files—by default, those files are MPEG-4 AAC files (Advanced Audio Codec), which can be played back in iTunes and on Apple's iPod.

NOTE *One thing you might notice in the previous paragraph is that iTunes does not, by default, create MP3 files, as you might have guessed if you know something about MP3s and digital music. iTunes creates AAC files by default, which take up a little less storage space than MP3s. iTunes can create MP3s, however. It only requires a simple setting change, as discussed in the "Set Encoding Options" section of this chapter.*

Importing songs from an audio CD is simple:

1. Select the CD in the source list.

2. Click to *remove* the check mark that's next to any of the songs in the list that you don't want to import.

4	☑ Keeping Quiet	5:15	One & Twenty	Don't Remember Fa...	Rock
5	☐ I Wish You Were Dead To Me	6:02	One & Twenty	Don't Remember Fa...	Rock
6	☑ Another Winter's Day	5:21	One & Twenty	Don't Remember Fa...	Rock

3. Click the Import button in the top-right corner of the iTunes window. This begins the import process.

In the status area, information about how the import process is proceeding will appear. You'll see the song's import progress grow along the indicator bar as well as information about the time remaining and the speed at which the import is taking place. (The speed indicator tells you how much faster the import is than the speed at which the song would play—*7x* means iTunes is importing the song seven times faster than it would take to play the song.)

While a song is being imported, you'll see a small orange squiggly circle next to the name of the song. Once successfully imported, a green circle with a check mark inside will appear beside it.

| 7 ⊘ | ☑ Comfort | 4:51 |
| 8 ◌ | ☑ Atlas (W/ Whipping Post) | 13:24 |

By default, iTunes will begin playing the songs that it's importing after it's gotten through the first one—to change that behavior, choose iTunes | Preferences and click the Importing button. Click to remove the check mark next to the option Play Songs While Importing. Click OK and, in the future, your songs will import in silence. (They'll also import quite a bit more quickly, so turning off this option is definitely recommended if importing the songs is more important to you than listening to the songs at that moment.)

Once songs are imported, you'll find them in the library. Just click the library icon in the Source list and you'll be able to see your new songs mixed in with earlier acquisitions. If you've got more CDs, then, as the shampoo bottles say, "rinse and repeat"—insert the new CD, remove the check mark next to any songs you don't want to import, and click the Import button.

Set Encoding Options

By default, iTunes does a fine job of importing songs from CDs to audio files in your library—but that doesn't mean you might not want to tweak settings every now and then. The default settings for iTunes create songs that are basically indistinguishable from CD quality audio and yet are designed not to take up too much space on your hard disk once they're imported. You can dig in and change those settings if you'd like to create audio files that are either of higher quality or of larger file size.

To make those changes, choose iTunes | Preferences and click the Importing button in the Preferences dialog box. You'll see the window shown in Figure 1-3.

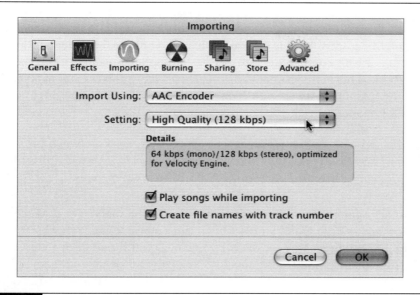

FIGURE 1-3   The iTunes Preferences dialog box

By default, if you're running QuickTime 6.2 or later with iTunes, you'll see
that iTunes is set to use the AAC Encoder, which is a high-quality file format and
codec that creates great-sounding audio files that take up relatively little disk space
for storage—about 1MB per minute of song. This is great for hard disk storage
and for transferring to CDs and other media. However, it might be a little large if
your goal was to send the file as an e-mail attachment or, in some cases, store the
file on an external digital music player. (This sized file would be fine for an iPod,
but a digital music player with considerably less capacity might be better off with
songs that require less storage space.)

NOTE   *The word codec means compressor/decompressor and refers to technology
that can make a digital file smaller than it otherwise would be. In most
cases, compressed files must be decompressed at the time they are played.
Applications such as iTunes (and consumer electronics devices like CD
players and iPods) are designed to do this.*

So your first option in the dialog box is to select a different encoder. Which should you choose? If you want to use your music primarily in iTunes and/or on an Apple iPod, then AAC is a good choice. The only real problem with AAC format is that it isn't compatible with devices or applications that are designed for MP3 playback. This includes many third-party portable players and most types of digital audio jukebox software you'll encounter. In such cases, you might want to select MP3 Encoder from the Import Using menu.

 *You can also choose AIFF Encoder or WAV Encoder, although you probably aren't as likely to do this unless special circumstances warrant it. See the following "How To" sidebar for details on these formats.*

Your other option is to make a selection in the Setting menu. For AAC encoding, this menu is set to High Quality (128 kbps). But you can change that by selecting Custom in the Setting menu. (For the MP3 Encoder, you'll find three settings—Good Quality, High Quality, and Higher Quality. You can choose among them or you can select Custom to make a customized choice.) Choose Custom and the Encoder's customizing dialog appears.

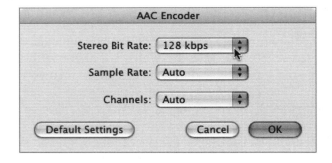

In this dialog, you can choose a Stereo Bit Rate from the menu—the higher the bit rate, the more data is used to describe the sounds recorded in the audio file. To a point, that means a higher-quality reproduction. It also means that the file used to store the audio is larger whenever you select a large bit rate and smaller when you select a smaller bit rate. Apple recommends 128 kbps for AAC files, although some users suggest 160 or 192 kbps for better sound reproduction. Numbers beyond that probably aren't necessary, but you can experiment with them.

The other options are probably best left set to Automatic, but you can change the Sample Rate if you'd like to fix it at either 44.100 KHz (which means 44,100 samples per second) or 48.000 KHz (48,000 samples per second). 44.100 KHz is CD-quality.

Finally, if you want to force iTunes to encode files as either stereo or mono, you can make that selection in the Channels menu; otherwise, leave it set to Auto. And when you're done in the dialog box, click OK.

> **NOTE**   *Much of the time, you'll be changing settings in this dialog box when you want to limit the file size of the files that iTunes creates when it imports a CD track. In that case, settings such as 64 or 96 kbps, 44.100 KHz and Mono might make more sense. Such recordings are close to AM radio quality, but the files are much smaller and might be ideal for transmitting over your Internet connection via e-mail or another method.*

How to ...   Understand Audio File Technology

I'm throwing a lot of acronyms at you in this section—MP3, AAC—and some techno buzzwords that we should master before moving on. These acronyms generally represent *file formats*—different ways in which computer files can be written and stored. iTunes can deal with audio files saved in any of these formats, but each has its strengths:

- **MP3**   You may already be familiar with this term—it stands for MPEG Layer 3 (MPEG, in turn, stands for the Moving Picture Experts Group) and it refers to a file format and method of compressing such data. MP3 became a popular moniker because it was the first codec/format scheme that got high-quality audio into files that are small enough to trade over the Internet. Although the "boom" in music trading that violated copyrights has subsided somewhat, the popularity of the format and the notion of good-quality audio files is still with us and has fed the popularity of iTunes, iPods, and other devices that make use of digital audio.

- **AAC**   Of course, progress can't be stopped, so the current master of the digital audio format—particularly in Apple products—is AAC, or Advanced Audio Codec. Developed by Dolby Labs, AAC is the audio component of the MPEG-4 standard, which is a popular multimedia file format and compressor for Internet-based video movies. AAC compresses slightly better than MP3 while maintaining the same overall quality. The difference isn't dramatic, but it's handy—a 128-kbps AAC file is considered on a par with a 160-kbps MP3 file, meaning the AAC file will be smaller at a similar quality level. (Note that not all AAC files are based on the MPEG-4 standard, so you may sometimes encounter a file that's called an "AAC" file, but won't playback in iTunes. That may be because it's based on technology that iTunes doesn't support.)

- ■ **WAV** This file format was the early Windows and DOS standard for audio files and it's still very much in use by audio-editing applications in Windows and on other platforms. WAV files can be used in much the same way that MP3 or AAC files can, but they're much larger. In most cases, you'll encode your CD tracks as WAV only if you intend to use them in other Windows music or digital audio editing applications.

- ■ **AIFF and AIFC** The Audio Interchange File Format and the AIFF-Compressed standards are essentially the Mac versions of WAV—file formats which create relatively large files that offer good playback reproduction but that aren't terribly portable. Again, most Mac digital audio editing applications can work with AIFF/AIFC files.

In fact, importing your audio tracks as WAV or AIFF would be the preferable approach if you intend to edit them in a digital audio application of some kind *before* encoding them as MP3 or AAC. We'll touch on that more in Chapter 9.

Add Audio Files to the Library

Now that you know that iTunes can create audio files—MP3, AAC, WAV, and AIFF—from CD tracks, it's worth noting that you can add existing files in those formats to your iTunes library very easily. There are a few different ways to do it.

NOTE   *Adding digital audio files to iTunes in this way—simply dragging them to the library—does not import them into the format that you've set in iTunes Preferences. In other words, an AIFF file will remain an AIFF file even after it's added—it isn't automatically translated into AAC or MP3, even if that's what you've set on the Importing screen in iTunes Preferences. You can, however, convert a song that's in your library—see Chapter 7 for details.*

The simplest approach to adding songs is almost too simple—drag and drop:

1. In iTunes, make sure the library has been selected in the source list.

2. Drag the audio file's icon from the desktop or a Finder window to the main list in iTunes (see Figure 10-4).

3. Drop the icon on the list. It will be imported into the library as if it were encoded from a CD.

TIP   *You can stop a file that's being encoded or imported by clicking the small "X" button that appears in the information area next to the progress indicator.*

The other way to add digital audio files is to choose File | Add To Library from the menu. That launches an Open dialog box, which you can use to navigate to the digital audio file(s) that you'd like to add. Select the file(s) in question and click Open. They will be copied to your library and will appear in the list.

FIGURE 1-4   To add a compatible audio file to the library, drag it to the library's list.

NOTE *By default, moving files to the library causes them to be copied into your default library folders. If you don't want to copy the files, but still want to access them from within iTunes, choose iTunes | Preferences and click the Advanced icon. Turn off the Copy Files To iTunes Music Folder When Adding To Library option and click OK. iTunes will now allow you to manage those files using the library listing, but will keep them in their original location. (See Chapter 2 for more on managing the library and locating individual song files.)*

Window Controls

The last thing I want to touch on briefly regarding the iTunes interface is its window controls. While the Mac and Windows version of iTunes can look nearly identical at first blush, this is one area where they differ somewhat, so we'll look at each separately.

Control the Mac Version

In the Mac version, the window controls are located at the top-left corner of the window. From left to right they are the Close (red), Minimize (yellow), and Maximize (green) buttons.

Clicking the Close button will close the iTunes window, but not the applications. You must select iTunes | Quit to quit the Mac version. Otherwise, the application will still be active. To see the iTunes window again, choose Window | iTunes.

Click the Minimize button and it does what it does in any Mac application—places the iTunes window on the Dock, where you can click it again to bring the window back up for access.

Click the Maximize button and the iTunes window will do something that most other Mac applications won't—the window will actually become smaller (and not maximized), transforming itself into a small player that you can position on your screen and use to access the basic controls in iTunes. (See Chapter 7 for more on this controller mode.)

Click the Maximize button again to return to the full iTunes window.

Control the Windows Version

1

In the Windows version of iTunes, the window controls are on the top-right side of the window. They are, from left to right, Minimize, Maximize, and Close.

Click the Minimize button and iTunes is minimized to the taskbar; click its entry on that taskbar and you'll see the full window again. Click the Maximize button and the iTunes window turns into the smaller player interface shown earlier in this chapter in the section "Control the Mac Version." It's discussed in more detail in Chapter 7. Finally, click the Close button in iTunes for Windows and you'll close *both* the iTunes window *and* the iTunes application, which is the default behavior in Windows.

Chapter 2

Organize the Library and Playlists

How to...

- Manage Your Songs
- Locate Your Stored Audio Files
- Search and Browse the Library
- Consolidate and Maintain Your Library
- Create a Playlist
- Build a Smart Playlist

The most obvious reason to use iTunes is to play back music and other audio files, which you saw how to do in Chapter 1. But once you get more than a few songs in your iTunes library, you'll likely find it's good to know a little something about how to organize them. Here in Chapter 2, we'll dig a little deeper into music playback and discuss how to handle individual songs once you have them in the iTunes interface.

Beyond just playing music and audio, the magic of iTunes is in how it enables you to organize, manipulate, and manage your music. After all, it's the promise of easy organization and access that's probably your main reason for putting music on your computer in the first place. With your music stored in the iTunes Library, you can easily search and browse for songs, artists, and albums. It will give you a whole new of way looking at your music collection.

But what if you don't *want* to deal with your entire collection of music all at once? Well, that's what playlists are for. You can create playlists to organize your favorite music for use on various occasions—whether it be working out, paying bills, or treating your love to a candlelight dinner. You can even use playlists to more conveniently export your music to portable digital music players. Indeed, the playlist is an incredibly important tool in the iTunes arsenal for organizing your songs—so we'll give them their due in this chapter.

NOTE *It's worth noting that by "songs," we really are talking about an audio file that you can play back via iTunes. "Song" is just easier to use than "digital audio track" or something similar. I mention this because I want to differentiate it from digital audio files, which are the computer files that we dig through outside of iTunes. In fact, we'll cover that in the section "Locate Your Stored Audio Files" later in this chapter. For now, we'll use the term "songs" even when we're talking about, say, tracks of spoken-word audio or audio book chapters.*

2

Manage Songs in iTunes

In the previous chapter, you saw how to select and play songs and audio tracks from CDs and how to get those songs from your CDs or compatible audio files into iTunes. In this section, I'd like to look at some of the different ways to manage and access song files in the main list, whether you're viewing them in the library, on a CD, or in a playlist (which you'll learn about later).

Sort the List

When you're viewing a list of songs, whether in the library, a playlist, or on a CD, you can sort that list in order to look at it in different ways. At the top of the main list are various column headings—Song Name, Time, Artist, and so on—all of which are items you can base your sorts upon.

Song Name	Time	Artist	Album	Genre	My Rating	Play C
☑ Go Away	3:04	Cramer	Cramer	Rock		
☑ Better Off Alone	2:41	Cramer	Cramer	Rock		
☑ Mercy Me	2:37	Cramer	Cramer	Rock		
☑ Thanks Again	2:51	Cramer	Cramer	Rock		
☑ Because Of You	3:35	Cramer	Cramer	Rock		

To sort by a particular column, simply click that column's heading. When you do, the list will reformat itself so the songs are sorted according to that particular column heading.

Song Name	Time	Artist	Album	Genre	My Rating	Play C
☑ Another Winter's Day	5:21	One & Twenty	Don't Remember Fa...	Rock		
☑ April In Paris	1:56	Marc Shaiman	Forget Paris – The ...	Soundtrack		
☑ April In Paris	6:35	Louis Armstrong	Forget Paris – The ...	Soundtrack		
☑ Atlas (W/ Whipping Post)	13:24	One & Twenty	Don't Remember Fa...	Rock		
☑ Bass Line	4:27	One & Twenty	Don't Remember Fa...	Rock		
☑ Because Of You	3:35	Cramer	Cramer	Rock		

When you click a column composed primarily of names or words, it will be sorted alphabetically—when you choose a column that's chiefly numbers (such as the Time column), it will be ordered according to the times listed. In both cases, you can change the sort order—whether items are sorted from higher to lower or vice versa—by clicking the same column heading a second time. (The list is sorted in ascending order when the small triangle points up, and in descending order when it points down.) When you do this, the triangle indicator will point in the opposite direction and the items' order will be reversed.

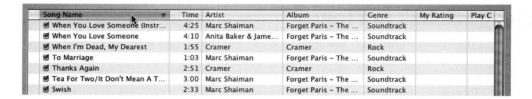

Sorting the list can be useful for locating a particular song, but it's also handy for changing the order in which songs are played. If you sort by artist in your library, for instance, you can hear all the songs by a certain artist before moving on to the next artist alphabetically; sort by Album to begin listening to all of the albums that you've imported, and in alphabetical order to boot.

Change the List's Columns

By default, iTunes shows you a number of columns in its lists, including those that appear when you view the library or a playlist. You can change the columns that appear in each of those lists, if desired. To change the library, for instance, make sure it's selected in the Source list and then choose Edit | View Options from the iTunes menu. This brings up the View Options window.

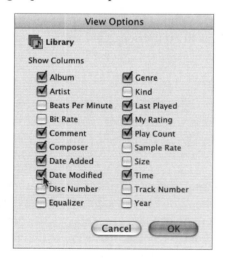

Now, click to place check marks next to the columns you'd like to see in the list, and click to remove check marks next to columns you don't want to view. When you're done, click the OK button. That should change the columns shown in the list immediately.

All playlists, including those generated by iTunes (My Top Rated, Recently Played, and so on) can have their columns set individually—select a playlist and choose Edit | View Options for each playlist you'd like to change.

CDs work a little differently; if you change the columns that show for one CD, those same column choices will be used for subsequent CDs you insert. You'll also notice that CDs have slightly fewer choices for columns than the library and playlists.

TIP *Want to change the order of the columns in the main list? To do this, hold down the* OPTION *key on a Mac or the* ALT *key in Windows, then click and hold the mouse button down while dragging the column left and right. As you drag, you'll see spaces open up between the columns where you can relocate the column you're dragging. To place the column there, release the mouse button.*

Edit Song Information

iTunes stores information about all of the songs that you import into the program, as well as songs that it encounters when you insert an audio CD, even for the songs that you don't import. If you want to change that information, you're free to—you can even rename songs, artists, and albums, or add information you don't currently have about a song.

Edit in the Info Window

The easy way to see all of the relevant information about a song is to select it in the main list and then choose File | Get Info. (You can also select a song and press ⌘-I in Mac OS X or CTRL-I in Windows to open this window.) Key information about the song is stored on the Info tab; click Info to see a screen that lets you make fairly extensive changes (see Figure 2-1).

Anything can be tweaked or changed on this screen. To change something, simply click its entry box and make changes using your keyboard. When you're done, click the OK button to put those changes into effect.

The Info box has other tabs, too—the Summary tab, for instance, can be used to learn quite a bit about a song at a glance. For an imported song, you'll see the file type (MP3, AAC, and so on), the size of the file, the bit rate, and other specifics. You'll also see the name, artist, album, and any artwork you have associated with the song (see Figure 2-2).

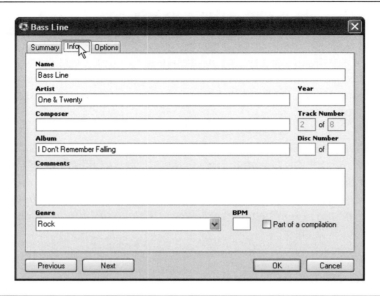

FIGURE 2-1 In the Info window, the Info tab is where you can make a lot of changes (Windows screen shown).

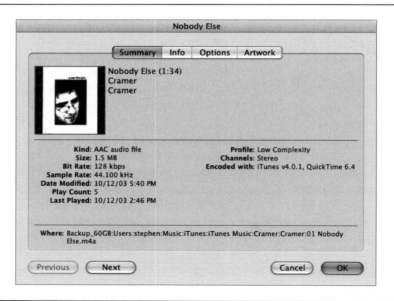

FIGURE 2-2 The Summary tab can tell you a good deal about a song (Mac OS X screen shown).

The Option tab offers you the ability to make specific choices about how this individual song will play. You can adjust the volume for a song that's too loud or soft when it plays back compared to others

in your collection; the Start Time and Stop Time features can be used to make a particular song begin playing late (using Start Time) or stop early (using Stop Time). Place a check mark next to one or both if you want them to be active.

You can set a rating for the song by clicking the My Rating box; click the small dots to place stars for your rating. The more stars, the higher the song's rating (in your opinion). iTunes notes these ratings and puts the top rating-getters in the My Top Rated playlist. You can also create your own "smart" playlists that take advantage of the My Rating settings.

Note also that while you're working in the Info window, you can use the Previous and Next buttons to move between the various tabs and click the OK button to put your choices into action.

Edit in the List

You can make changes to your songs directly within the main list if you'd prefer not to open an Info window for each song you want to edit; of course, in the list, you're limited to the columns you can see. (To see more columns, access Edit | View Options, as I mentioned in the section "Change the List's Columns.") To edit any item you see in a column, first make sure that the song has been selected (highlighted) in the list. Then, click the name or other item you want to edit—it should become highlighted, allowing you to use the keyboard to make changes.

☑ Point Blank		2:38	Cramer
☑ When I am Dead, My Dearest		1:55	Cramer
☑ Fun Is Free – Acoustic		2:13	Cramer

Not all entries are changed using the keyboard; if you have the My Rating column showing, you can change the rating for a song using your mouse. Click to highlight the song in question, then click in the My Rating column to set a rating for the song—again, the small dots act as your guide to set a "star" rating indicating how much you like a song.

☑ Fun Is Free – Acoustic	2:13	Cramer	Cramer	Rock	★★★★
☑ Before It Rains	4:10	Cramer	Cramer	Rock	★★★
☑ Never Come	4:24	Cramer	Cramer	Rock	★★★★
☑ Sleep	3:07	Cramer	Cramer	Rock	★★
☑ Beekman Place	5:26	One & Twenty	Don't Remember Fa...	Rock	★★★
☑ Bass Line	4:27	One & Twenty	Don't Remember Fa...	Rock	★★★★
☑ Poor Ophelia	6:03	One & Twenty	Don't Remember Fa...	Rock	
☑ Keeping Quiet	5:15	One & Twenty	Don't Remember Fa...	Rock	

> **TIP**   *Is the My Rating column not currently visible? You can still change the rating; simply* CONTROL-*click in Mac OS X or right-click a song in Windows to bring up a contextual menu. Now, choose My Rating from the menu, then choose one of the levels in that menu. Notice that the contextual menu lets you access other commands, too, such as Get Info and the Convert Selection command.*

Get CDDB Info

Obviously, if you change something so it isn't true—for example, making yourself the artists for all your favorite songs—then you're limiting the usefulness of some of the searching and browsing tools we've discussed (as well as those discussed later in this chapter). But iTunes leaves it up to you. And the changes you make will be recognized and "believed" by iTunes—if you change all of your Billy Joel songs to Billy *Idol* songs, then searching for Billy Joel will probably net you nothing—even if you've got "Piano Man" and "Uptown Girl" sitting right there in your library.

You can, however, get the CDDB database to check a song or songs again and resupply the correct information—at least to the extent that it knows the correct info. You can also do this for songs that didn't get checked the first time for some reason—perhaps your Internet connection was down when you inserted the CD and imported the songs. To check, simply highlight a song or songs in the list and choose Advanced | Get CD Track Names. If you select more than one item, you may see a dialog box that asks you to confirm that you want to check multiple songs. Once you're past that, the database will be consulted and, if it has information about the original song or songs, the song name, artist, and album will be updated with the info in the database—and all your Billy Joel song info will be back.

View and Edit Artwork

Each song you import into iTunes can have artwork attached to it if you like. Songs you buy from the iTunes Store may already have the artwork attached, and you may have songs from other sources that include artwork. To view that artwork, click the song and choose Edit | Show Artwork. The result is a small window that appears beneath the source list, as shown in Figure 2-3.

If the song doesn't have artwork associated with it, you can add some in one of two ways. The first method is via the Get Info window:

1. Select a song and choose File | Get Info.

2. In the Get Info window, click the Artwork tab.

3. On the Artwork screen, you can either drag the image into the entry box or select Add. (If you drag the image into the box, you can click OK to move on.)

4. An Open dialog box will appear; locate the image file and click OK to add it for this song.

5. Click OK when you've added the image.

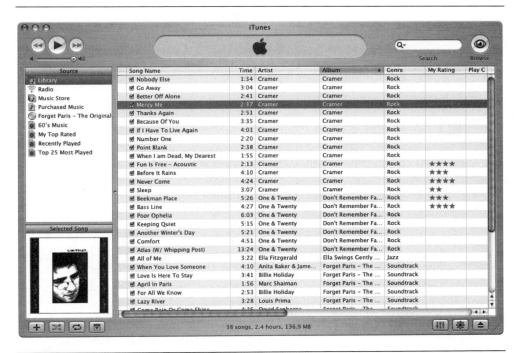

FIGURE 2-3   The artwork may include an album cover or whatever art is associated with the song.

The other way becomes apparent when you view a song that doesn't have artwork already associated with it. Here, you can simply drag an image from elsewhere on your computer into the empty image well.

To remove an image, go back into the Get Info window, select the Artwork tab, and then choose the image and click the Delete button. Click OK in the Get Info window and the artwork will be removed.

Note also that you can have more than one image associated with a song at a time—simply drag more images into the image well or into the box on the Artwork tab in the Get Info window. When you have multiple images, you can scroll through them using the small left and right triangle controls that appear above the artwork in the iTunes window.

 *You can double-click the artwork in the iTunes window if you'd like to see a larger version of that image.*

Delete Songs

Though it sounds unlikely, you may one day want to delete a song from your library or from a playlist. (You can't delete songs off a CD, although you can delete them from external digital music players—something that's also discussed in Chapter 8.) Deleting a song or songs is a simple matter—highlight the song(s) in the list and press the DELETE or DEL key on your keyboard or choose Edit | Clear. On a Mac, you can also drag the song(s) from the list to the Trash. You may see a dialog box that asks you if you're sure you want to delete the song(s).

Click Yes if you really want to delete the song(s) or Cancel if you've changed your mind. Notice that if you don't want to see this dialog box in the future, you can click to place a check mark next to the option Do Not Ask Me Again.

You may see another dialog box—this one asking whether you want music files moved to the Trash. (This only happens for files that were created or copied to your music folder by iTunes in the first place.) If you want them moved, click Yes; if you don't want them moved (but you still want them out of iTunes), click No. If you want to stop the whole process and not remove the songs from iTunes, click Cancel.

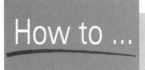 **Locate Your Stored Audio Files**

iTunes gives you plenty of ways to manage and manipulate your digital songs, but it requires an additional step for you to get at the underlying digital audio file, which you may want to access from time to time. If you're working with default settings and importing or copying the majority of your songs, then you'll likely find them in the Music folder inside your home folder on a Mac. In Windows, you'll find that iTunes stores files in your My Music folder.

Still, finding a particular song may take some digging. If, instead, you'd like to go directly to the source and locate a specific file, you can do that from within iTunes. Highlight the file in question and choose File | Show Song File. (You can also use a contextual menu—CONTROL-click on a Mac or right-click in Windows, then choose Show Song File.) That should cause the Finder window or Windows Explorer window to appear with the song's file highlighted.

Build Your Library Skills

As you add more and more songs to your library, you'll increasingly find it handy to view the library list in different ways. Believe me, scrolling through a few thousand songs can get tedious, even if you can sort the columns. To help you do that, iTunes gives you two distinct sets of tools, the Search and the Browse tools. We'll look at each in this section.

Search the Library

Actually, searching works in any kind of a list in iTunes, including a playlist or a CD, although searching those lists isn't quite as useful or necessary, since they tend to be shorter lists compared to the full library. You can also search for radio stations or search the iTunes Music Store—we'll cover those eventualities in the appropriate chapters.

For now, let's focus on the library. Searching is a two-step process that you perform using the Search box at the top-right corner of the iTunes interface. First, you select the criteria to which you would like to limit your search. You do that by clicking the small magnifying glass on the left side of the search box and then selecting a criterion from the menu that pops up.

Next, type a keyword. You'll notice that, as you type the keyword, the search begins and the list of songs shown in the main list will dwindle somewhat. Only the songs that match your keyword—even the first few letters as you're typing— are shown (see Figure 2-4).

You'll find that the list is much easier to work with after it's been whittled down by even a few letters; once you get to a full name or word, it should be relatively easy to scroll through the rest of that list.

When you're ready to see the full list again, click the small circle with an "X" in it at the right side of the search box. That removes the keyword (or letters) you typed and returns the view to that of the entire list.

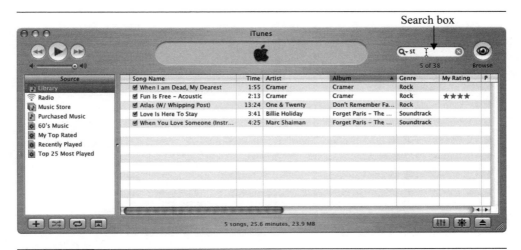

FIGURE 2-4   As you type a keyword, the list dwindles.

Browse the Library

Browsing is different from searching—instead of simply whittling down the list to a few songs, browsing helps you get a different perspective on your collection of music, particularly if it's a reasonably extensive collection. Browsing lets you look at your songs in different ways, whether by genre, artist, album name, or a combination thereof. It's a fun way to look at an extensive collection, as well as an interesting way to help you build playlists and group your music, as you'll see in the sections later in this chapter.

For now, though, let's browse. To get into browse mode, click the Browse button at the top right corner of the iTunes interface. That changes the configuration of the iTunes window so it looks like Figure 2-5. (You can also get into browse mode by choosing Edit | Show Browser or by clicking ⌘-B in Mac OS X, or CTRL-B in Windows.)

With the Browser window up and active, you're free to click around to get different looks at your songs. Each of the columns—Genre, Artist, and Album—acts as a filter for the list that appears below them. Using the columns, you can slowly whittle the list down to as many or as few songs as you'd like to see. Browse helps you not only get to a particular song or set of songs (the way Search does), but it also lets you see the different types, artists, and albums you have.

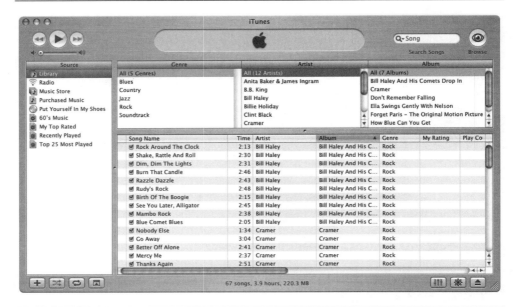

FIGURE 2-5 After you click Browse, the iTunes window rearranges itself.

Begin in the Genre column, where you can choose a particular genre if you'd like to see only songs in that genre, or where you can click All to keep from filtering the songs. You can select multiple genres if you like. Simply hold down the ⌘ (Mac) or CTRL (Windows) keys as you click additional genres. When you select one or more, you'll notice that the list in the Artist column changes—it's filtered down to the artists that fit that genre.

Once you've chosen a genre, you can select an artist (or multiple artists) to see the albums that you have by the artist(s). Finally, you can select an album and you'll see a list of songs on that album in the list area below the columns. Along the way, though, you can see tons of different and interesting things—select a genre

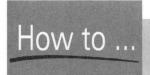

Consolidate Your Library

Once you've been working with your library for a while, you may end up with songs that are stored in a variety of ways—some may have been copied to your music folder, while others may be stored elsewhere on your disk, in a shared folder, on a network volume, external disk, and so on. If you prefer to have all of those music files in the same place, you can consolidate your library. To do so, simply choose Advanced | Consolidate Library from the iTunes menu. This will cause any digital audio files that aren't already stored in the default iTunes music folder to be copied to it. Depending on the size of your library and the number of stray audio files, this can take a little while. (Note: iTunes doesn't check to make sure your hard disk has enough space to copy any and all digital audio files to your iTunes folder. You should check for free space yourself first, or you may fill your disk and encounter a "disk full" error during the consolidation process. See Chapter 8 for more.)

without selecting any artists and you'll see all of the albums for that genre in the Album column and, by extension, every song in that genre shown in the list below the columns. Or, if you view all genres but select an artist or artists, you can see all of their albums and songs, regardless of the genre. And so on.

When you're done browsing, click the Browse button again. (You can also choose Edit | Hide Browser, press ⌘-B on the Mac or CTRL-B in Windows.) The iTunes interface will reconfigure once more and you're back to the full listing of your library.

As you might have guessed, all of the information that iTunes uses to help you browse your songs can be edited using the Info window discussed earlier in the section "Edit Song Information."

Organize with Playlists

While you can search and browse your full library of songs, the playlist is the utmost in convenience for organizing your songs for daily use. As the name suggests, a playlist is a list of songs designed for playback—a subset of the songs in your library that you can create to decide what, exactly, you want to listen to.

You can create one list for working, one for working out, one for yoga, one for hanging out and doing nothing—each of which can be formed from the songs in your library, arranged and then listened to countless times. What's more, multiple playlists can have the same song on them—in fact, all the songs remain in your library even after they're added to playlists. The playlists are simply references to the song files that you've stored and can access using iTunes—they're your opportunity to arrange your songs however you'd like them played.

Beyond those basics, playlists can do quite a lot, as you'll see in later chapters. For instance, if you decide to burn an audio CD of songs, you'll create a playlist and arrange the songs for that CD before the burning process begins. If you're working with an iPod or an external digital audio player, you'll also be working with playlists (you may just want to do this for organizational purposes) and so on. Beyond that, playlists themselves can be a bit more sophisticated—iTunes enables you to create a *smart playlist,* which can change based on the criteria and logic you set.

Create a Playlist

To create a playlist, click the plus (+) button at the bottom of the source list or choose File | New Playlist from the iTunes menu. (You can also press ⌘-N on a Mac or CTRL-N in Windows.) When you do, an untitled playlist appears with the name highlighted. You can begin typing immediately to name the playlist.

When you're done typing, press RETURN and the playlist will take on the new name. The next step is to drag songs to it—dig into your library, by scrolling or searching or browsing, and drag song files from the library to your new playlist. You can drag a single song or multiple songs to the playlist icon and drop them there to add them to the playlist. (To select multiple songs, hold down ⌘ on a Mac or CTRL in Windows while clicking song titles.)

	Song Name	Time	Artist	Album	Genre	My Rating	Play Co...
Top 25 Most Played	☑ Rock Around The Clock	2:13	Bill Haley	Bill Haley And His C...	Rock		
Work Tunes Rudy's Rock	☑ Shake, Rattle And Roll	2:30	Bill Haley	Bill Haley And His C...	Rock		
	☑ Dim, Dim The Lights	2:31	Bill Haley	Bill Haley And His C...	Rock		
	☑ Burn That Candle	2:46	Bill Haley	Bill Haley And His C...	Rock		
Mambo Rock	☑ Razzle Dazzle	2:43	Bill Haley	Bill Haley And His C...	Rock		
	☑ Rudy's Rock	2:48	Bill Haley	Bill Haley And His C...	Rock		
Nobody Else	☑ Birth Of The Boogie	2:15	Bill Haley	Bill Haley And His C...	Rock		
	☑ See You Later, Alligator	2:45	Bill Haley	Bill Haley And His C...	Rock		
	☑ Mambo Rock	2:38	Bill Haley	Bill Haley And His C...	Rock		
	☑ Blue Comet Blues	2:05	Bill Haley	Bill Haley And His C...	Rock		
	☑ Nobody Else	1:34	Cramer	Cramer	Rock		
	☑ Go Away	3:04	Cramer	Cramer	Rock		
	☑ Better Off Alone	2:41	Cramer	Cramer	Rock		

Create Playlists in Alternative Ways

Bored with the same old methods of creating a playlist? Well, you can actually use a few shortcuts to create those playlists a bit more quickly. And if anyone is looking over your shoulder, they'll think you're an iTunes wizard.

You can select the songs for a playlist first, if you'd like, and then create the playlist with those songs in it. Highlight the songs you want to add to a playlist in the library—use the ⌘ key on a Mac or the CTRL key in Windows as you click to add songs to your overall selection. Once you've selected all the songs you want to add to the playlist, choose File | New Playlist from Selection or press ⌘-SHIFT-N (Mac) or CTRL-SHIFT-N (Windows). The new playlist will be created just as it normally is, except that it's already got the selected songs in it.

Oh—and you don't even have to use the New Playlist From Selection command. With songs highlighted in the library, simply click and drag one of them to the source list—all of the other highlighted songs will come along for the ride. Drop those songs in a blank portion of the source list (make sure no other playlists or devices are selected by your hovering mouse pointer). When you release the mouse button, the selected songs are added to a new playlist that iTunes attempts to name automatically.

Once you've got the songs in the playlist that you want, you can click the playlist in the source list to switch to it. Now, the first thing you'll likely want to do is drag your songs into a new order—setting the order is one of the key advantages of using a playlist. To change a song's order, simply click it and drag it to a new location in the list. As you drag, a thin black line shows you where the song will appear in the list when you drop it. (Note that when you drag a song to a new location, the numbers for all songs in the list change to reflect the new order.)

▲	Song Name	Time	Artist	Album
1	☑ Rudy's Rock	2:48	Bill Haley	Bill Haley And His C…
2	☑ Mambo Rock	2:38	Bill Haley	Bill Haley And His C…
3	☑ Nobody Else	1:34	Cramer	Cramer
4	☑ Lazy River	3:28	Louis Prima	Forget Paris – The …
5	☑ See You Later, Alligator	2:45	Bill Haley	Bill Haley And His C…
6	☑ Paris Suite	6:12	Marc Shaiman	Forget Paris – The …
7	☑ Love Is Here To Stay	3:41	Billie Holiday	Forget Paris – The …
8	☑ When You Love Someone	4:10	Anita Baker & Jame…	Forget Paris – The …
9	☑ Beekman Place	5:26	One & Twenty	Don't Remember Fa…

As with any other list in iTunes, you can click a column to sort the list as well. In addition, notice that whenever you sort the list by clicking a column header, you are again changing the sort number of the songs in the list.

Want to play the songs in your list? Select a song and click the Play button or press the spacebar. You can manage playback (as described in Chapter 1) just as you would with any list, using the Repeat and Shuffle tools, if desired.

To remove a song from a playlist, select it and press the DEL key on your keyboard or choose Edit | Clear from the menu. You may then see a dialog box asking you to confirm your decision; click Yes to delete the file. (Note that you can click to place a check mark next to the Do Not Ask Me Again option if you don't want iTunes to show you dialog boxes when you delete songs in the future.) When you delete a song from a playlist, it's not deleted from your library.

To delete an entire playlist, select it in the source list and press the DEL key (or chose Edit | Clear or CONTROL-click (Mac) or right-click (Windows) the playlist and select Clear from the menu). If you have songs on that playlist, you may see a dialog box asking if you're sure you want to delete the playlist; click Yes if you are. (If you don't have songs on the playlist, it's deleted immediately.)

You can export a playlist as a text file if you'd like a list of the songs in a computer file. Choose File | Export Song List. In the Save dialog box, choose a location, a format (Plain Text, Unicode Text, or XML), give the file a name, and click Save.

Smart Playlists

A smart playlist is one that can accomplish things automatically—in iTunes, Apple has already included a few smart playlists such as the Recently Played and My Top Rated playlists. These playlists are constantly updated whenever you do something in iTunes—if you play a new song, the Recently Played playlist is updated; if you change the rating for a song, the Top Rated playlist might change (assuming you gave the new song a high enough rating).

Creating a smart playlist, as you might imagine, is also a little more involved than creating a regular one. To begin the process, choose File | Create Smart Playlist. A dialog box appears:

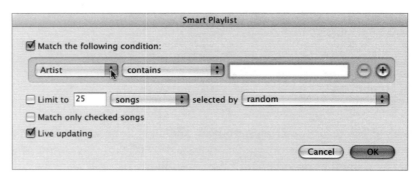

It's in the dialog box that you'll create your smart playlist. What you're essentially doing is building a search phrase, telling iTunes that if it finds a song that meets the following criteria, put it in this playlist. You build the criteria using the menus and entry boxes. To see the options, click the first menu in the criterion section of the dialog box.

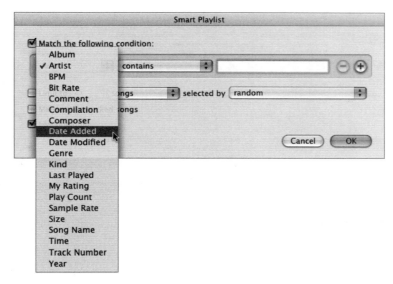

Each criterion will start with the first menu, and will generally have a second menu and an entry box that comes after that first menu. What you're essentially doing is building a little sentence; the first menu is a noun (Artist, Bit Rate, Composer), the second menu is a verb (is, is not, contains), and the third is the object of the sentence—whatever it is that you're comparing it against.

As an example, consider a smart playlist that would show all songs over 4MB in file size. Here's how it would work:

1. Choose File | New Smart Playlist.

2. Make sure a check mark appears next to Match.

3. From the first menu, choose "Size," and from the second, choose "is greater than" and enter **4** in the entry box.

4. Make sure Live Updating is enabled.

5. Click OK.

6. When the playlist appears, begin typing to give it a name and press RETURN when done.

FIGURE 2-6 The Big Songs smart playlist is listing songs that are over 4MB, as it was told to do.

Now, if you select this playlist in the source list, you'll see the songs that match the criterion show up in the main list (see Figure 2-6).

A smart playlist can get considerably more complicated—you can add more criteria, for instance, by clicking the Plus (+) button to the right of your first criterion. With multiple criteria available, it makes it possible to create a smart playlist that shows songs that are over five minutes long and are in the blues genre. (See the end of this section for other ideas.)

When you add more criteria, the Match item changes—a menu is added. In that menu, you can choose whether the playlist will match All or Any of the criteria. Matching "All" will limit the playlist only to those songs that meet all the criteria—it's like putting "And" between each criterion statement. Matching "Any" is like putting the word "Or" between each of the criterion.

The smart playlists will only be limited by your imagination—and by the other three items in the Smart Playlist dialog box. Click the Limit To _____ option if you'd like to add a criterion that's designed to limit items in the smart playlist. You do this by adding a check mark, choosing something from the first menu (songs, hours, megabytes), and selecting something from the second menu to determine how the limited number of songs are to be selected. In fact, you could disable the first set of criteria (the Match option) and work only with the Limit line.

You've already seen how the Live Updating works—it it's not selected, the playlist won't update on the fly, but will remain with the same songs that it listed the first time it ran. Finally, the Match Only Checked Songs option does what it says—it won't compare the criteria against songs that aren't checked in your library.

As you might already have guessed, the possibilities for smart playlists are fairly broad—anything you can think of that has to do with the information found about a song in the Info window in iTunes can be used to automatically build a playlist. And that playlist can be used for playback in iTunes, it can be burned to a CD, or even exported to your iPod—anything you can do with a regular playlist you can do with a smart one. Here are a few brainstorming thoughts to leave your with regarding smart playlists:

- Use the Genre criteria to automatically create playlists that only include songs in certain genres. You can augment such lists with other criteria, such as a list that includes only classical Genre songs where the Time is greater than 6:00.

- Use the Bit Rate criteria to create playlists that separate your songs into higher and lower quality recordings. (See Chapters 3 and 9 for more on bit rates.)

- Choose Year is 1967 to hear songs that were made when you were born (or when you graduated high school).

- Try Song Name contains a certain word to create themed playlists—"Love" or "Lady" or "Night" or "Walking" might come up with a fun playlist that includes all different types of songs that have a common theme in their title.

■ Turn *off* the Match the Follow Condition criterion and you can use the Limit To criterion to create playlists of your highest or lowest rated songs, your most or least often played songs, and so on.

You can likely come up with many more once you get a sense of how these playlists work and why they're enjoyable to work with.

Chapter 3

Burn CDs and DVDs

How to...

- Burn an MP3 CD
- Burn a Data CD or DVD
- Use Tips and Tricks When Burning
- Troubleshoot Problems
- Use Third-Party Burning Solutions

It's nice having all your music in one place in iTunes, but what do you do if you want to take some of it with you? One solution is to burn your own CDs if your computer has the capability. When burned in audio CD format, you can play your CD full of songs in pretty much any CD player, whether a consumer player, a CD player in your car, or a CD-ROM drive on another multimedia computer. In fact, iTunes enables you to create CDs from playlists you create in iTunes, meaning you can put together all sorts of "mix discs" of your favorite songs, regardless of the artist or original album.

The audio CD format is handy, but iTunes offers other options as well. You can, for instance, burn an MP3 disc—one that features MP3 files instead of audio tracks. Some of today's consumer CD players—particularly car stereos and portable CD players—can play these files just as they do CD audio tracks. The advantage is that you can fit a whole lot more songs on an MP3 CD than you can on an audio CD. iTunes also allows you to create data CDs, which are similar to MP3 CDs except that they can house song files other than MP3s. This type of CD is best for backing up your audio library or for playing it back exclusively on a computer.

Finally, we'll take a quick look at a third-party option for burning CDs and why you might want to consider it.

Burn Audio CDs

Audio CDs are convenient because they're so easy to play back under a variety of conditions. These days, you can be fairly certain that you'll encounter a CD player in your travels, so if you want to take your songs with you to a party or a presentation or in a rental car, then an audio CD is probably the way to go. Plus, what's more fun than mixing your own CDs on your computer for use in the "offline" world?

What You Need

Burning CDs in iTunes requires a few different things. First, you need a drive that's capable of burning CDs, whether it's built into your computer or connected to it externally. Such drives are those that can create discs in the CD-R or CD-RW formats; you may have a straight CD-RW drive, or one that can both read DVDs and burn CD-RW discs, for instance, or you may even have a drive that can burn both DVDs and CDs. (On Macs, these are called "SuperDrives," and on Windows PCs, they're known as DVD-RW or DVD+RW drives.) Table 3-1 may be helpful in understanding all these formats.

In most cases for audio CDs, you'll probably want to write to CD-R media, because it's less expensive and it's more reliable for playback in a variety of consumer electronic devices. Because of the difference in the dyes used to "burn" data to the disc, CD-RW can be a little more difficult for some CD playback devices (particularly consumer and car stereos) to read, especially if they're a few years old. CD-R can also have problems with very old CD players, but most contemporary ones aren't an issue. For audio CDs, burning to a CD format is necessary; you can use DVD media for backup and for data discs.

Type of Drive	Definition	Description
CD-R	CD-Recordable	Refers to a drive that can write one time to a recordable CD. CD-R also refers to media that can only be written to ("burned") once.
CD-RW	CD-Rewriteable	Refers to drives that can write to either CD-R or CD-RW media. CD-RW media can be written to, erased, and written to again.
DVD-R	DVD-Recordable	"Write once" DVD recording technology.
DVD-RW	DVD-Rewriteable	DVD-RW drives can write to either DVD-R or DVD-RW media. The DVD-RW media can be erased and written to again.
DVD+R, DVD+RW	DVD+Recordable and DVD+Rewriteable	DVD+R and DVD+RW (note the +) are standards that are similar to, but distinct from, DVD-R and DVD-RW; DVD+R/+RW support is more common on PCs than Macs.

TABLE 3-1 Various Drive Types and Their Descriptions

iTunes can work with many, but not all, CD-R or similar drives. In order to burn discs, you're going to need a drive that is compatible with iTunes. If it isn't compatible, you probably can't burn CDs from within iTunes. Instead, you'll have to work with a third-party application. The easy way to find out if your CD/DVD drive is iTunes compatible is to ask the manufacturer or check its materials. The second easiest way is to consult www.apple.com/macosx/upgrade/storage.html for Mac compatibility and visit www.info.apple.com/usen/itunes/windows/ for information on drives in Windows. (I haven't actually found a topic on that page that's specifically about compatibility, but the page hasn't been up all that long at the time of this writing.)

The CD-RW drive built in to any Mac model should be compatible with iTunes. (One notable exception is the DVD-RAM drive in some Power Macintosh G4 models, which can't write to CD-R or CD-RW media.) For PCs, the newer the drive and the more recognizable the name brand, the better.

Burn a Playlist

When you burn an audio CD, you're actually writing in the standard format that's recognizable by regular CD players so that the CD player itself doesn't have to be aware of the difference. iTunes has this capability built in, as long as you've got a compatible CD-R (or better) drive.

To begin, you should create a playlist in iTunes that contains the songs you want to burn to your audio CD. You'll probably want to create a new playlist to start your CD—click the Plus (+) button at the bottom of the source list or choose File | New Playlist to start your list, then give it a name (consider carefully, as it will be the name of the disc you're burning). With the playlist created, begin dragging songs to it from the library. You'll notice at the bottom of the iTunes window when you're viewing your playlist that iTunes keeps track of the number of songs and the amount of time those songs take up.

On an audio CD, you've got 74 minutes (80 minutes on some discs) you can fill. While some audio CDs are a little longer than billed, you probably don't want to push it too close since you may encounter a problem or lose part of a song. Also, the order of the songs is important—you should drag the songs around and listen to each if you want to make sure the transitions sound good and that the songs fit well back-to-back.

When you have the songs arranged the way you want them, and you're ready to burn the CD, click the Burn Disc action button in the top-right corner of the iTunes window. You'll see the button reconfigure into a glowing nuclear-warning style symbol. If you don't have a disc in the drive, the Please Insert Blank Disc message will appear in the information center in iTunes. On many models, your CD player will automatically open. Insert a blank CD-R in the drive and close it.

Next, iTunes will check the media and compare it against your playlist. If your playlist is too long, you'll get an error message from iTunes:

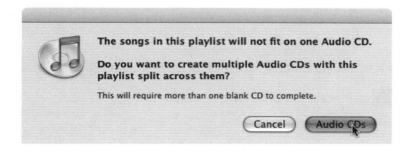

Click the Audio CDs button if you don't mind spilling over onto additional discs (and you have some more CD-Rs available). If that's not an appealing proposition, click Cancel and whittle down your list.

If iTunes figures that your playlist will fit on the CD you've inserted, you'll see the information area blink the message Click Burn Disc To Start. Click the Burn Disk button again to start the burning process. The progress will be reported in the information area of the iTunes window. Depending on your drive's speed, it should take, in minutes, anywhere from half the length of your playlist to a fifth or less of its total time to burn the songs to the CD (see Figure 3-1).

NOTE   *While iTunes is burning a playlist to a CD, you can't make changes to that playlist. Makes sense, eh?*

Both Mac OS X and Windows XP are capable of allowing you to work on your computer while a disc is being written to—but I still don't recommend it unless it's an absolute necessity. Even if it doesn't happen often, it's still possible for an errant

FIGURE 3-1 iTunes burning a playlist to an audio CD

application or another problem to slow down or interrupt the write process, even temporarily. When that happens, you may end up with a write error that causes the burn process to stop or which adds an error to the disc.

> *One important factor necessary for a smooth burning session is RAM— the more RAM you have in your computer, the more likely you are to have a successful burn and, more to the point, the greater the chance you'll be able to continue using your computer while the burn is taking place. If you have a lot of trouble burning CDs from iTunes, consider upgrading your RAM.*

If all goes well, the disc will be burned, finished up, and then it will be mounted within iTunes, ready for you to play just like any other audio CD (see Figure 3-2).

FIGURE 3-2   The CD has been burned and is ready for playback.

Audio CD Options

Not happy with the way the audio CD burn happens by default? You can make some choices in the iTunes Preferences that affect audio CD burning. Choose iTunes | Preferences and then click the Burning icon.

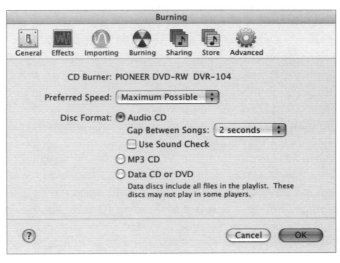

There are three basic options you can change that will affect your audio CD burn. First, you can choose a setting from the Preferred Speed menu. By default, the choice is Maximum Possible, but you might want to choose a different speed if you frequently have problems burning CDs. If you encounter errors, you can try dropping back to 8x or slower (depending, in part, on your drive's age) to see if that helps.

With the Audio CD radio button selected, you have two other options. First, you can choose an amount of time from the Gap Between Songs menu; the longer the amount of time you put here, the less cross fade there is between each song. By default, when set to None, the second song will begin playing just as the first one ends; the longer the delay, the more "dead space" there is between each track. (Even at the default, the gap can seem somewhat lengthy. In my experience, None works just fine for this setting.)

> **NOTE**   *If you want songs that you're importing from a CD to have no gap at all, the best bet is to choose two or more tracks on that CD and select Advanced | Join CD Tracks in iTunes. This causes iTunes to see multiple CD tracks as one track when they're imported so they have the original gap (or lack thereof) that the CD had. Of course, with one big track, it makes it tougher to listen to individual songs in iTunes—but if you're looking for a better reproduction of the CD to CD-R, this feature might be helpful.*

Finally, you can choose to use Sound Check information for burning this CD. This is only useful if you're prepared for it, however. As discussed in Chapter 1, if you have Sound Check turned on in the Effects preferences, then whenever you import a song, iTunes will make note of its volume level. You can then use the Sound Check feature to make sure that songs play back at generally the same level. If you're already making use of that feature, then turning on this option in the Burning preferences means that the Sound Check feature will also be used when burning the CD—in other words, iTunes will do what it can to equalize the volume level of the songs that you're burning.

When you're done setting preferences, click the OK button in the dialog box.

> **NOTE**   *Having trouble burning a music CD that includes tracks you bought from the iTunes Music Store? With protected AAC files, you should know that you need to rearrange a playlist after you've burned it to CD ten times. Just go in and change the order of the songs and/or move some out and add some new ones into the playlist. Then, go ahead and burn that newly arranged list. Apple does this to cut down on CD piracy.*

Burn MP3s and Data CDs

Creating audio CDs is quite a feat, but that's not all that iTunes is capable of. You can also use iTunes to record MP3 CDs, which can be played back in many consumer CD players. You can also create data CDs of your song files, which are best used for the backup and transfer of your library.

> **NOTE** *Burning an MP3 or data CD can be a good solution if you happen to be low on hard disk space. This way, you can store hundreds of songs and play them directly off the CDs in iTunes. Also, with data CDs, you can actually burn a playlist that's larger than the CD can handle and iTunes will prompt you to enter a second CD when it's necessary, making the transfer of a large number of songs relatively easier.*

Burn an MP3 CD

If you want to get more songs on a CD, you'll sometimes find that burning an MP3 CD is the way to go. When you do that, your songs are placed on the CD in the compressed MP3 format instead of the larger Audio CD tracks. This can be a huge advantage since you can generally get up to 12 hours of songs on a single CD. There are caveats, however, and they're somewhat severe. First, in order to be played back on consumer equipment, the equipment needs to specifically support MP3 playback. Not just any CD player can handle this—it needs to be designed specifically for it. Many of today's CD components for stereo systems (as well as many DVD players, as it turns out) can handle MP3 CDs as well.

The second issue may be more of a challenge, particularly for Mac users: you can only burn *MP3s* to an MP3 CD. Sounds obvious. The problem is that iTunes 4 and later defaults to AAC as the digital music format. So, when you import songs from a CD or buy them from the Apple iTunes Store, if you have your import encoder set to AAC in the Importing pane of the iTunes Preferences dialog box, you won't be able to burn those files to an MP3 CD without first translating them into MP3s. Fortunately, iTunes 4.1 and later allow you to translate a file that you've imported to MP3 format—select the song in the main list and then choose Advanced | Convert Selection to MP3. After a moment, the song will be converted and a second copy (the MP3) appears in your library.

So, if you've got MP3s in your library and you'd like to burn them to a CD, you can do it and it's fairly straightforward. Here are the steps:

1. Open iTunes | Preference and click the Burning icon.

2. Open the Burning pane, select MP3 CD, and click OK.

3. In the iTunes interface window, create a playlist in iTunes by choosing File | New Playlist or clicking the Plus (+) symbol beneath the source list.

4. Drag any and all MP3s to the playlist that you'd like to burn to the MP3 CD. (iTunes can actually look at a playlist and burn *only* the MP3s, so if you drag over some AAC or music files in other formats, you'll be OK.)

5. Arrange the items on your playlist as desired.

6. Click the Burn Disc button.

7. If a blank recordable CD isn't already in your drive, you'll be asked to insert one. Do so and iTunes will prepare for the burn. If you've included non-MP3 songs in your playlist, you'll see a dialog box. Click OK to continue.

The burn happens. Watch the info area at the top of the window for progress as the MP3 CD is burned. When it's done, you'll have a CD on the source list that you can access and use for playback—after all, these are MP3s, which iTunes can handle with aplomb. Now, eject the CD and take it with you for playback on other computers or in an MP3-enabled CD/DVD playback unit.

Burn a Data Disc

When you burn your songs to a CD or DVD as a data disc, any sort of digital music files—MP3, AAC, AIFC, WAV—recognized by iTunes and stored in your iTunes Library can be stored on the disc. You may have noticed something else operative in this description—you can use DVDs. The combination of compressed digital music files (as opposed to audio CD tracks) and high-capacity recordable DVD media means you can get thousands of songs on a single disc—the equivalent of 150 CDs, according to Apple. So, it makes a data disc a great option for backup.

The steps for creating a data disc should be fairly familiar:

1. Begin by choosing iTunes | Preferences and clicking the Burning button.

2. Select the Data CD or DVD option and click OK.

3. Create a playlist, give it a name (it will be the disc's name), and drag over all of the files you want to burn to this data disc.

4. Check the text at the bottom of the iTunes window for an indication of how large the playlist is—for a CD, your maximum is about 700MB; for a DVD, the limit is around 4.7GB.

5. Eject a disc if there's one in your computer's drive.

6. Click the Burn Disc button. You'll be prompted to insert a disc—do so and wait for the information window to tell you to click Burn Disc again.

7. Click Burn Disc again.

Now, sit back and allow the burn to happen—it may take a while, particularly if you've got a large library and you're burning a big chunk of it to DVD. When you're done, once again you'll have a disc that's mounted in iTunes which you can play the songs from as if they were stored on your computer's hard disk. There are relatively few consumer playback devices that can handle data discs created in iTunes, but you may be able to play those songs on other computers. (Of course, that's made easier if you're using iTunes on those other computers, but other digital music applications should be able to play most of these files as well.)

Third-Party Burning Solutions

iTunes is capable of doing most of what you're interested in accomplishing when it comes to burning to disc, but if you have additional wants or needs, you may want to look into a third-party solution. We'll look at two in particular in this section: Roxio Toast for Macintosh and Roxio AudioCentral (part of Easy CD/DVD Creator) for Windows.

> NOTE
>
> *There are plenty more options out there, but the Roxio entries are the two most popular. For Mac, try CharisMac's Discribe (www.charismac.com) for burning audio CDs, data CDs, and even for MP3 and AAC translation (see Chapter 7 for a closer look). For PC, try Nero 6 (www.nero.com/en/ index.html). Remember, too, that both Mac OS X and Windows XP can burn data CDs from within their operating systems.*

Roxio Toast

After iTunes itself, the most popular option for burning CDs on a Mac is Roxio Toast. Toast is capable of doing quite a bit—it can burn data CDs in Macintosh, Windows, and hybrid formats and it can burn Audio CDs while offering an extra option or two compared to iTunes.

The Roxio Toast window (shown in Figure 3-3) is designed to be accessible and easy to use. To create a Data CD, for instance, simply click the Data button and choose from the menu the format you'd like to use for the CD. (For instance, you

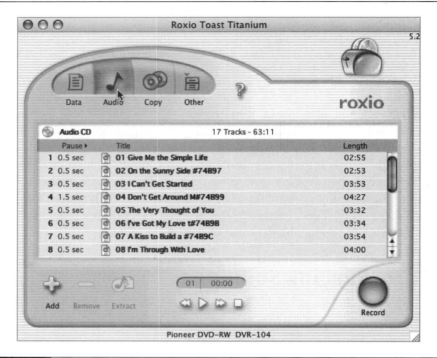

FIGURE 3-3 Roxio Toast for Mac OS X

can choose a Mac OS CD, a Hybrid, a Mac OS Extended CD, and so on.) Then, drag files to the window in order to add them to the list of those you'd like to burn, or choose File | Open and use the Open dialog box to locate files and folders that you want burned to CD (for instance, files and folders inside your iTunes Music folder).

 *Toast can be used to write to a data CD in different sessions, meaning you can write more than once to the same CD-R (or CD-RW without erasing) until it's filled. That can be handy, particularly for backups.*

Toast can be used specifically to create audio CDs. Click the Audio button in the interface to start the process. Toast's ability is similar to that of iTunes—you drag some songs into the window, which acts as a playlist for your CD. You can drag the songs around to rearrange them. Note in the window how much time the songs will consume and how many tracks they represent. Toast goes a little beyond iTunes in a few details—for instance, in Toast, you can set the exact length of the pause between each individual track. Click the entry in the Pause column for a particular song to bring up a small menu where you can change the settings.

Click the name of a song to edit it in the list, which you may need to do because Toast can alter long song names, adding numbers and symbols (see Figure 3-3). Use the keyboard to edit the name and press RETURN (for Mac) or ENTER (for PC) when you're done.

Toast gives you some extra utility features compared to iTunes—for instance, before burning a CD, you can choose Utilities | Check Speed to get Toast to the individual songs in your playlist in order to make sure it won't have any trouble burning them at a given speed. Click Test All to get the lowdown on the complete playlist or select a particular track and click Test to see how it will burn.

You can even test a burn in simulation mode before going through with the final pass—this is handy for older Macs or slower drives that exhibit trouble in iTunes. Choose Recorder | Simulation Mode and then click Record in the Toast window. Toast will go through the entire burning process once you click the Write Disc button. If you don't have any troubles, you can unclick the Simulation option and click Write Disc again, this time for real.

That's a quick look at Toast. For more on Roxio tools for Mac, see Chapter 7, which discusses recording and editing digital audio files.

Roxio AudioCentral Player (CD/DVD Creator) for Windows

For dealing with digital audio files, Roxio CD/DVD Creator for Windows offers a tool called the AudioCentral Player that, in some ways, acts a lot like iTunes. When you first launch it, you're asked if you'd like to add any songs to the AudioCentral media library. If you say yes, your disk will be searched for compatible music and other files. You'll then see a window that looks something like Figure 3-4, which you can use for playback, just as with iTunes. Select a song and click the Play button to play it. By default, you'll even see visualizations of the music in the AudioCentral window.

FIGURE 3-4   The AudioCentral interface playing a song.

To build a playlist so that you can create an audio CD, select the songs you want on that playlist and then right-click one of the selected songs. In the menu that appears, choose Add To Playlist. You'll see a dialog box that enables you to choose the playlist you want to add the songs to, or you can use that dialog to create a new playlist, which you can then name by typing in the appropriate text.

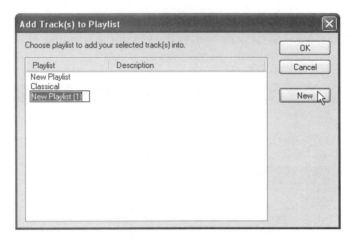

Click the playlist to which you want to add the songs, and then click OK. The songs are added to that playlist. You can return to the library and add more songs in the same way, or you can switch to the playlists to see and manage them. To switch to playlists, choose View | Track List View | Playlists. The Track List View (the "drawer" on the side of the Audio Central controller window) will reconfigure to show you playlists.

Now that you can click and drag songs around on the playlist to change their order, you can also select a song. Right-click and you'll have access to tons of options that you won't find in iTunes, such as the capability to Edit Playlist Audio Effects or Edit Transitions. In fact, the latter is very cool—it enables you to very specifically edit the gaps and overlays between songs in your playlist, allowing you to create a very custom-sounding set of transitions between songs on the CDs that you burn. (You'll have to play around with it a little, but it makes sense pretty quickly. Note that you have the option, at the top of the window, of using the same transition as the current track for all subsequent songs.)

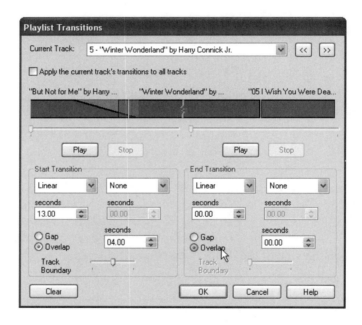

When you've made all the settings you want to make, you're ready to burn the CD. You can do that by selecting the Burn icon in the AudioCentral window (it's the orange-yellow CD with flames coming out of it), or you can choose File | Burn Track List or press CTRL-B. Whatever approach you take, you'll bring up the Burn Setup window shown in Figure 3-5.

Here, most of the default selections have been made for you, but you can tweak the settings if you like. In the Disk Format menu, you can choose to burn a data disc instead of an audio disc, for instance. You'll see in the bar below that option the amount of spaces that will be taken up on the disc. Note that you can choose the burner you want to use from the Destination menu if you have more than one burner.

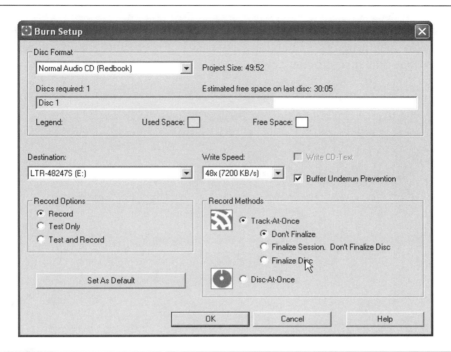

FIGURE 3-5   The Burn Setup window

You can also choose the burn speed in the aptly named Write Speed menu. It's best to only lower this if you're having trouble at the default speed. In the Record Options section, you have the option of choosing Record To The Disc, Test Only (which means you won't actually write to the disc), and Test And Record, which will do both.

Perhaps the most intriguing options are the Track-At-Once and Disc-At-Once options. Disc-At-Once may be more familiar to you since it's the way iTunes and other applications tend to burn audio CDs, by creating an entire disc and finalizing it in one operation. After it's written to once, you're done writing to it. With Track-At-Once, however, you can choose to write a few audio tracks to a CD and then choose Don't Finalize. When you do, the CD is left open so you can record additional tracks to it. If you're interested in listening to the CD, but you still want to write to it, choose Finalize Session, Don't Finalize Disc. When you've chosen the final songs you want on the CD and you're ready to burn it, choose Finalize Disc.

With those choices made, you're ready to burn. Click the OK button. The software will take over and begin burning your CD. Click the Show Details button to see more as it progresses, including any errors or problems. Otherwise, sit back and wait until the disc is done.

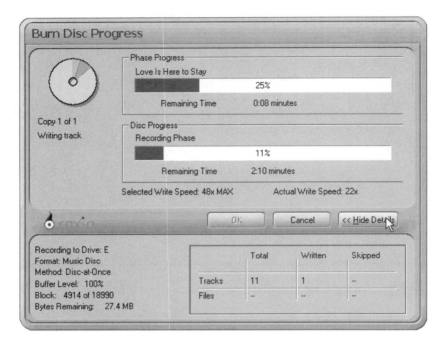

Chapter 4

The iTunes Music Store

How to...

- Use the iTunes Music Store
- Get Signed Up
- Browse the Store
- Search the Store
- Sample the Music
- Make a Purchase
- Play Back and Use the Song

While I've found iTunes handy for managing songs imported from music CDs for a while now—particularly for the music I play when I'm working in my office—when the iTunes Music Store was launched, I was impressed, partly because I hadn't been fond of the whole MP3 "swapping" scene. The idea of being able to buy exactly the songs I wanted for a reasonable price was cool. Up until the Music Store, I hadn't been much of an "online MP3"–type person—I was more focused on playing and organizing the songs I already had. (If you have been an MP3-swapper, here's your chance to go legit!)

Using the iTunes Music Store, I've discovered a whole other world that goes beyond simply paying for songs and downloading them over the Internet. Perhaps the best part of the Music Store is the many ways you can browse and search for music. Although the iTunes Music Store database represents a relatively small share of all recorded music, it's growing constantly and may one day be a formidable—perhaps even the authoritative—music catalog. (And that may happen sooner than we think.) Already, you can do some amazing things just by searching: find songs with similar titles, find the same songs recorded and covered by different artists, or uncover all the songs in the catalog done by a particular artist.

Once you find a song you like, you can listen to a high-quality, 30-second clip. That's the real secret to online shopping—where in the real world can you do that when shopping for songs? Given this opportunity to dig and prod and learn more about music, coupled with the instant gratification offered by the iTunes Music Store, it's no wonder it's been called "iCaffeine" (and similar sarcastic monikers based on harsher drugs) thanks to its addictive qualities.

In this chapter, we'll take a look at the iTunes Music Store, including how to manage it and get the most out of your time there. To start, though, we'll discuss the technology behind the store, the songs themselves, and just what, exactly, you're buying.

Get Started

At the Music Store, you can jump in and begin searching for, and buying, songs very quickly—but there's a thing or two you should know first. And once you understand these concepts, you're ready to sign up.

Understand the Music Store

When you access the Music Store via your copy of iTunes, you're really signing on to Internet servers that run web-based applications designed to manage the appearance of the store, the specials, the searches, and the purchasing process. The iTunes Music Store is the same whether you access it from a Mac or a Windows-based PC—it's really no more than a typical web site. The difference is that iTunes is the required browser—that way, the store's interface can fit in well with the iTunes interface you're already familiar with.

NOTE *At the time of writing, the iTunes Music Store could only be accessed from within the U.S.—those visiting the store with a non-U.S. IP address are redirected to a page that tells them the store won't work unless they have a credit card with a U.S. billing address. For some, this will likely end in the near future, perhaps before you read this, since it's expected that Canadians and Europeans will have access to the store relatively soon.*

The point of the iTunes Music Store is to enable you to buy individual digital music files of professional, published music. In most cases, each digital music file represents a track from a CD. Currently, Apple sells these tracks for $0.99 a piece, and will sell entire albums for various prices, usually so that each song is a little less than $1.00. What you get in return is a "protected" AAC file—it can be burned to a CD and transferred to your iPod, but taking it to a different iTunes Library requires your iTunes account name and password. Doing this authorizes the song for your particular computer. You're allowed to authorize up to three computers, so it's something you'll need to think about when trying to play back songs—even shared songs over network connections. (We'll discuss this in more depth later in the section "Play Purchased Songs.")

NOTE *The iTunes Music Store isn't all about songs. With the introduction of the iTunes Music Store for Windows came the addition of AudioBooks, which are essentially the "Books On Tape" versions of popular novels and non-fiction that have been saved in AAC formats and which can be downloaded to your computer. The books, of course, are more expensive than the songs, and they take a lot longer to download, but they're still an intriguing addition and, what's more, they're convenient to work with if you'd like to listen to audio books on your computer or via an iPod.*

Part of what's amazing about the iTunes store is the various ways you can search and browse the Music Store. This is because it's a sophisticated database that's being queried by your iTunes software. When you search for a song title, you'll get a listing of all the songs that come close to that title. When you find a song that looks interesting—whether you've searched or browsed or just happened upon that song—you can click and listen to a clip of that song. You can also click an icon next to the album or the artist's name to dig further into the Music Store database and find other songs on that album, or other work by that artist.

If you like what you hear, you can buy the song (or the album, or the audiobook) on the spot. All you have to do is register and give your credit card number to Apple. Once you've done that, you'll have the option of using a "one-click" technology to buy all your future songs.

When using the Music Store, you can definitely benefit from a broadband Internet connection. If you use a dial-up modem to access the Internet, you may end up a bit frustrated when trying to sample songs, download purchased songs, or take advantage of some of the extras such as the music videos and longer-length samples.

Get Connected and Signed Up

To get started with the Music Store, first connect to the Internet if your access requires you connect initially. Then, click the Music Store entry in the Source list. You'll see a progress indicator in the information window and the iTunes window will reconfigure itself so you're looking at the main Music Store window (see Figure 4-1).

You don't have to register immediately upon entering the Music Store; although you will be asked to register occasionally, you don't have to do so until you decide to buy something—as long as you're just shopping, Apple doesn't need to know who you are. Once you decide to take the plunge and buy a song—or if you'd like to get the registration process out of the way—click the Account Sign In button at the top-right of the Music Store interface.

When you do that, or if you click to buy a song, album, or other item in the Music Store and you're not signed in, the Sign In dialog box will appear. If you have an Apple ID (say, if you've bought from the Apple Store before or paid for a .Mac account), you can sign in immediately by entering the Apple ID and Password in their respective entry boxes and clicking Sign In. If you don't have an Apple ID,

FIGURE 4-1   A typical home page from the Music Store

click the Create New Account button and you'll be guided through the process of signing up for an ID, which includes agreeing to the Apple Account legal agreement, entering the required personal information, and entering your credit card and billing information.

Once you're signed in, you'll see your e-mail account in the top-right corner. That e-mail address is actually a link which you can click to get to a screen that shows your personal information and where you can make changes to your account information, password, address, or your credit card information. You can also use the Apple Account Information screen to work with features such as Gift Certificates and Allowance. When you're finished managing your account, click the Done button at the bottom of the page.

The other thing that having your e-mail address in the top-right corner tells you is that you're ready to purchase some music—for as long as your credit card can handle the purchases, that is.

To sign out of the iTunes Music Store, click your name again—you'll see the Enter Password dialog box. Instead of entering your password, click the Sign Out button in that dialog. When you do that, you're signed out of the store—now, if another person wanted to, he or she could enter another Apple ID and Password using this same copy of iTunes.

> NOTE *Working with more than one Apple ID can get a little complicated. If you buy a song with ID #2 in the same copy of iTunes that's been used before with ID #1, then that new song, licensed to ID #2, will be placed in the library and authorized on this computer. Now, ID #2 could be authorized on up to two other computers, and they won't necessarily be the same computers as those authorized by ID #1. In other words, you could find yourself in a situation where some of your songs will play on one machine and not another. (See the sidebar "How to…Understand iTunes Authorization" later in this chapter.)*

Find and Buy Songs

iTunes offers a few different ways you can track down the songs you're interested in. This includes browsing, searching, and special features such as celebrity playlists and lists of top sales. Once you've found the song, album, or other audio file you'd like to buy, you can do it easily.

Browse the Store

There are a number of ways to browse the iTunes Music Store, starting with the most obvious: clicking links on the Music Store's home page, which Apple changes constantly to let you know about new releases and songs as well as best sellers and other choices and recommendations. On the screen as it's currently configured while I'm writing this, you can see such lists as Today's Top Songs, Today's Top Albums, Featured Artists, New Releases, and Celebrity Playlists. You'll also see the sections that Apple is probably most proud of—the Exclusives (stuff you can only get through the iTunes Music Store) and the Pre-Releases (songs you can get first on the Music Store before they're available anywhere else). To access one of these items, either click the artwork associated with it or click the name of the song or album—it's probably a hyperlink that, like a link on a web page, will take you to a new "page" within the iTunes Music Store interface.

Another way in which the iTunes Music Store interface is like a web browser is the toolbar that you're presented with at the top of the main list when you're in Music Store "mode." If you've spent some time surfing the Web, this will look at least somewhat familiar:

On the left side of the toolbar are the Back and Forward buttons. You can use these just as you would on the Web, to move around on the pages you're viewing. If, for instance, you're viewing an artist's page and you click one of the artist's albums to view it, you can click the Back button to return to the artist's page. You could then click the Forward button to return, once again, to that individual album's page. As in real-life Web use, you'll likely use the Back button more often—it's handy for backing all the way out of a browsing session if you want to return to a place you've been before.

To the right of the arrow buttons is a handy little control—basically a clickable "path" through the Music Store catalog that allows you to move to different pages fairly easily. There's a Home button (with the house icon) that you can click to return to the main iTunes Music Store page. The other buttons are also important since they show you where you are as you browse the store, and generally exist in the form of Home | Genre | Artist | Album, although you'll find variations. Click one of these buttons and you're taken to a logical new page—the Artist page, for instance, which will show you all the albums that the iTunes Music Store has for that particular artist (see Figure 4-2). The Artist page often also offers links to biographical information, as well as other fun lists, such as links to influences for this artist or others who have similar sensibilities (as well as other relationships). In fact, some Artist pages can get pretty involved, particularly if Apple has an exclusive on those artists, or features music videos or publicity photos for the same.

> **NOTE** *Some artists do have full-length music videos available that you can watch using QuickTime technology. If you don't have a fast Internet connection, you might want to skip this content since it'll take a while to download and play. But broadband users can simply pick a size when presented with the option—a QuickTime window should appear within the iTunes list area, enabling you to watch the video.*

Another great way to browse the iTunes Music Store is by choosing a genre on the home page. Under the Choose Genre menu, you can select the genre you'd like to explore. After making your choice, you'll see a new "landing page," which, like the main Home page, will offer tons of top lists, recommendations, new releases, and other content, but all within that genre. This is a fun way to dig into the types of music you like and see what's being released, what's been added to the Music Store, and what's being recommended by Apple.

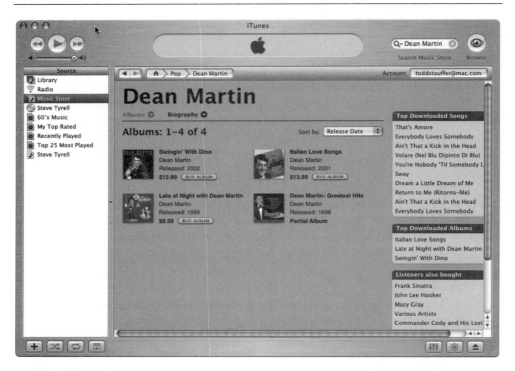

FIGURE 4-2 An example of an Artist page, where you'll find biographical details and links to additional information, such as other albums by the same artist.

Power Browse

Apple doesn't really call this feature the "Power Browse," but it's how I like to think of it. What you're essentially able to do is move through the iTunes Music Store using a browsing mode that's similar to the Browse mode in the iTunes Library. To get there, find the Browse Music link on the home page of the Music Store and click it. A window like that in Figure 4-3 will open.

Choose a genre in the Genre column and a list of artists will appear in the Artist column. Select an artist and you'll see that artist's albums in the Album column; choose an Album and you'll see songs appear in the list below the columns. In the song list, you can double-click a song to hear a sample of it, or click the small arrow icon next to the artist, the album, or the genre to leave the browse interface and go to the landing page for that particular item. (See the section "Sample the Music" for more on how to make use of these results pages.)

How to ... Link to a Song in the iTunes Music Store

Got a web site or a blog? A lot of personal web publishers like to post links to their favorite songs, albums, or bands on their web sites, whether to promote the band or just to share the experience. Apple makes it possible for you to add links on your web pages that will lead views to a particular song, artist, or album in the Apple Music Store.

How does it work? Just visit www.apple.com/itunes/linkmaker/ on Apple's web site. When you get there, enter the Song Name, Album, and/or Artist name, and then click Search. (You can enter one, two, or all three, depending on what you're trying to link to.) You'll then get a results list that you can search through to find the item to which you want to link. When you click that item, a screen appears telling you the HTML code you need to add to your page, including some scripting code that goes in the Head section of your HTML document and an anchor reference (the code that creates the hyperlink), which you can place in the body of your HTML document.

FIGURE 4-3   The browse interface for the Music Store lets you dig through music by genre and/or artist.

Search the Store

As with browsing, the Music Store interface offers two different ways to search for music—a simple way and a "power" approach.

Simple Search

With the simple search, you can enter keywords in the small Search Music Store entry box at the top-right of the iTunes interface. This is very similar to the search you can use for your own iTunes Library. Here's how to do it:

1. Select the criterion for your search by clicking the small magnifying glass icon and choosing from the menu that appears.

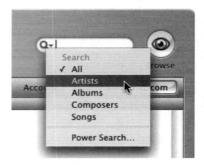

2. Enter the keyword, name, or whatever else might be appropriate for the criterion you choose and press Return to begin the search. (You can use just part of a name or keyword if you'd like to broaden your search—choosing "Artist" as the criterion and entering **Miss** as the keyword will bring up artists named both "Missy Elliot" and "Mississippi John Hurt.")

3. Press Return. This step isn't required in the regular iTunes search entry box, but in order to send your choices to the Music Store database, you need to press Return. When you do, your search results will appear in the list area (see Figure 4-4).

Notice that the search results will have a *Relevance* associated with them—the longer the bar in the Relevance column, the closer iTunes believes the match is to your keyword or words. It isn't always right—you may find it more useful to click one of the column headings to re-sort the list and look at it alphabetically by name, artist, or album, for instance. Most of the same tricks for viewing the main list that we discussed in Chapter 2 are relevant for this results list, as well.

Power Search

You'll find that the simple search is great for finding a particular song or artist, but it's more limited if you're looking to search more generally within genres, or if, for

FIGURE 4-4   Search results appear in the bottom half of the main list area; at the top are featured items based on your search criteria and keywords.

some reason, what you're looking for doesn't quite fit the simple search you can use the Power Search interface, which not only enables you to use multiple criteria at once, but also lets you experiment with different criteria and keywords, as you'll see. Here's how it works:

1. Click the Power Search link on the iTunes Music Store home page, or click the magnifying glass icon in the simple search entry box and choose Power Search from the menu.

2. The Power Search interface will appear, as shown Figure 4-5. At the top of the listing area are entry boxes for various criteria. Put a keyword in each of the boxes that interests you. You don't have to enter something in every box.

3. Choose a genre from the Genre menu if you'd like to include it as a limiting criterion.

4. Click the Search button to begin the search.

As you can see in Figure 4-5, the Power Search is really handy for cross-referencing different criteria—in the example, I'm looking for songs where Sinatra (probably Frank, but it could be Nancy or someone lesser known) has done songs by Gershwin. This interface allows for some fun experimentation since you can change the artist (How about Ella Fitzgerald's Gershwin songs?) or the composer (try Sinatra's Cole Porter renditions) or you might search for a particular song and

FIGURE 4-5 The Power Search, complete with some keywords and results

limit its genre. Has the song "I'll Be Seeing You" ever been arranged in a classical music style? Or as an R&B tune? Has Elton John's "Rocket Man" ever been done as a New Age song? (Yes, by John Tesh. It's…interesting.)

That's the power, and fun, of the Power Search. Click the Cancel button to return to the iTunes home page at any time.

Sample the Music

OK, so you've either browsed or searched and you now have a listing of songs you'd like to check out. Let's look at those listings a little more closely.

The typical results lines look something like this:

While the City Sleeps	3:53	Chicago	⊙	Chicago V	⊙	▮▮▮▮▮▮▮▮	$0.99	BUY SONG
State of the Union	6:15	Chicago	⊙	Chicago V	⊙	▮▮▮▮▮▮▮▮	$0.99	BUY SONG
Goodbye	6:05	Chicago	⊙	Chicago V	⊙	▮▮▮▮▮▮▮▮	$0.99	BUY SONG

Here are some of the things you can do with that result:

■ Double-click the result and you'll hear a 30-second sample of the song.

■ Click the arrow icon next to the Artist name and you'll head to the landing page for that artist—generally, you'll see the artist's albums, bonus tracks, top downloads (and perhaps biography), articles, and even music videos from that artist.

■ Click the arrow icon next to the album name and you'll be sent to that album's page. There you'll get a list of all the songs on that album; you may also see cover art and a write-up about the album if it has one.

■ Click the Buy Song button and you'll launch the purchasing process (see the next section, "Make a Purchase").

■ Click one of the column headers to change the way that the list is organized and presented to you. Click Song Name to see the list alphabetized by title; click Artist to see the list arranged by artist name, and so on.

In a list of songs, you can also use the playback controls (the VCR-like controls in the top-left corner) to hear the 30-second samples of each clip. To move between them, use the Forward and Back double-arrow icons, or click the Play/Pause button to play or pause (whichever is appropriate). Of course, the volume slider can be used to change the volume level when playing back a clip.

TIP *Playing song-by-song in the iTunes Music Store can get a little tedious, but there's no built-in way around that. There are, however, AppleScripts available for the Mac version of iTunes that enable you to play a list of song samples in the iTunes Music Store without being forced to launch each sample. See Chapter 10 for more on AppleScripts and for links to the best spots to find them on the Web.*

Make a Purchase

When you've found a song you like enough to add it to your library, Apple's that much closer to having you hooked. The next step is to click the Buy Song button that's associated with the song you want to buy. You'll also see Buy Album buttons on many album pages and Buy Book links on an audio book page.

Click one of these links and what happens next will depend on whether you have an account, and whether you're signed in to it. If you aren't yet signed in, you'll see a dialog box that asks you to enter your Apple ID and Password; if you don't have an Apple ID and password, you can select the Create A New Account option to input them. (See the section "Get Started" earlier in this chapter for details on how all this works.) Enter the necessary information and click Buy.

If you are already logged in, you'll see a dialog box that asks you to confirm your password—enter it and click Buy.

NOTE *The iTunes Music Store has "album" pages for those albums to which it doesn't offer all of the songs from. Sometimes (for rights clearance or whatever reasons), the iTunes Music Store is able to sell only certain tracks from a particular album. In such cases, you won't be able to click the button that lets you buy the whole album—instead, you'll see the words "Partial Album" to indicate that you can only buy individual tracks.*

When you click the Buy button, you'll see another dialog box. This one will ask you if you're sure you want to buy the song, album, or audio book that you've chosen. Click the Buy button again if you really want the item in question.

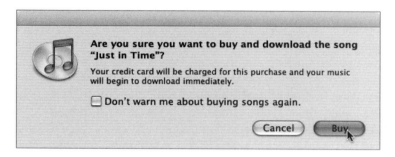

Note in this dialog box that you can also click to place a check mark next to the Don't Warn Me About Buying Songs Again option (it will also say "albums" or "audio books" if you're downloading one of those things). If you enable this option, the warning dialog box will not appear in future purchases.

NOTE *The next step is that the Apple Store will attempt to charge the credit card on file. If in the future the card is declined, a dialog box will ask you to input your password so you can change your billing information.*

If your billing information is correct, the transaction will go through and the information area will show that the purchased song is being downloaded to your library.

TIP *If you're having trouble with an iTunes purchase or have other questions about how the iTunes Music Store works, you can select Help | Music Store Customer Service from the iTunes menu. This will launch Apple's iTunes AppleCare web site, where you'll find articles and Q&As about various common problems and solutions. This is a quick way to access tutorial information and links that enable you to write Apple to offer your feedback or concerns.*

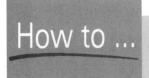 **Use the Shopping Cart**

The technique for buying songs discussed in this section is the "one-click" method, which purchases a song (or album) and begins immediately downloading it. This is the perfect solution for people like me—impatient people with broadband Internet access. But what if you've got a modem connection and/or you'd like to keep shopping instead of tying things up with the purchasing process? In that case, you can add items to your "shopping cart" and then purchase and download them all at once when you're done shopping.

So, how do you use the shopping cart? Open iTunes Preferences, click the Store button and choose Buy using a Shopping Cart. When you close iTunes Preferences, you'll find that the iTunes Music Store has changed—now, instead of Buy Song and Buy Album links, you'll see Add Song and Add Album links. Also, under the Music Store entry in the source list, you'll see a Shopping Cart, which you can select to view its contents.

When you're done making selections, you can choose the Shopping Cart entry in the source list to see a list of the songs you've chosen and their total price—the latter of which appears at the bottom of the list next to the BUY NOW button. Click the button to move on with the purchasing process.

Play Purchased Songs

When you buy a song from the iTunes Music Store, it's placed in your library with the other songs previously imported. To play it, do as you would with any other song—just double-click it in the list, or select it and click the Play button in the playback controls, press the spacebar, or select Controls | Play.

 Don't forget to back up your purchased songs either by burning a data disk or by copying them to a backup some other way. Once the song is downloaded from the Music Store, it can't be downloaded again without repurchasing it. See Chapter 11 for backup advice.

You'll also find your songs on a new playlist that's created when you buy your first song—the Purchased Music playlist. All the songs you buy from the iTunes Music Store (on this machine) are placed in the Purchased Music playlist, making it easy for you to check them out quickly, make sure they've downloaded properly, that the quality is good, and so forth.

NOTE *Having trouble playing a bought song? If you're concerned that you bought a song, album, or other file that wasn't completely downloaded, you can select Advanced | Check For Purchased Music and iTunes will access your accounts over the Internet and see if any songs you bought weren't fully downloaded. If it finds one, it'll let you know and the song will be downloaded immediately. You can also access Help | Music Store Customer Service to attempt to get help from an Apple representative. You should also watch your e-mail for a receipt from Apple which should show up within a few days of your purchase—if you never get one, it's possible the transaction wasn't completed.*

Transfer and Burn Purchased Songs

Although purchased songs can be played back the same way imported songs can, they are different from your typical imported MP3 or AAC files. The songs you download from the iTunes Music Store are Protected AAC files, which means two things—they can only be played back on computers that you authorize for playback and they can't be translated into other formats using iTunes. So, an AAC file can't be directly translated into an MP3 file, for instance, which may be important to you if you use an external MP3 player that isn't AAC compatible.

NOTE *iTunes makes this a little confusing because it offers the command Advanced | Convert Selection To AAC or Advanced | Convert Selection To MP3 and so on, depending on your settings on the Importing screen in iTunes Preferences. (Ideally, these commands wouldn't be selectable when protected AAC files were highlighted in iTunes.) The truth is, these commands don't work on protected AAC files, as you'll see if you try to convert them. If you do attempt it, a dialog box will appear, warning you that you can't.*

You can, however, use your purchased songs with up to three different computers (Macs or PCs), as long as you use your Apple ID and password to authorized their playback. Likewise, you can burn a CD from your purchased music, and mix and match purchased and imported songs on a playlist that can be used for burning CDs.

Transfer a Song

To transfer a song and use it on another computer, begin by moving the file from one computer to the other. To do this, use whatever technology you use for transferring other files from computer to computer—a local area network, an e-mail attachment, an Internet chat service or server, a removable disk, or even a data CD-R. When you're dealing with the digital music file itself, you may notice that its icon and description are a bit different; it's called an AAC Protected file and the icon has a tiny little padlock in it.

09 Just in Time.m4p

When you get the song to the target computer, you can then add it to that computer's iTunes Library using the methods discussed in Chapter 1—by accessing the File | Import command or dragging the file to the iTunes Library list and dropping it there. That adds the song to the library.

When you attempt to play the song the first time, you'll see a dialog box that asks you to authorize the computer to play this song if the computer hasn't already been authorized. (All you're doing is entering your Apple ID and Password and then clicking the Authorize button.) You can authorize up to three computers—if you already have this song authorized on three computers, you won't be able to play it on another one until you deauthorize one of your computers.

You may get in a situation where you don't know what Apple ID was used to purchase a particular song, which means you're not sure how to authorize it. You can find out by selecting the song in iTunes and choosing File | Get Info or pressing ⌘-I to bring up the Information dialog box. On the Summary tab, you'll see the Purchased By and Apple ID entries, which tell you what Apple ID needs to be used to authorize this song.

Deauthorize (and Reauthorize) a Computer

If you've reached your limit of three computers and want to deauthorize one so you can play your songs elsewhere, you can do it using the Deauthorize Computer

How to ... Understand iTunes Authorization

A computer can be authorized to play music from a particular Apple Account. Once authorized, any song associated with that account can be played on the authorized computer. Apple limits you to three computers that can be authorized at once, based on the logic that you might have up to three computers at home (or one at work and one at home and one in the vacation home or a laptop you carry with you) and you should be able to play your songs on all three of those machines without too much trouble.

Realize that it's not the individual songs that can be played back on three different computers—any song you buy using a particular iTunes account can only be played back (directly) on one of those three authorized computers. That's an important distinction—the entire purchased library is really managed as a whole by the authorization process.

If you've reached the limit—you've authorized three different computers to play the songs bought using a particular Apple ID—and you'd like to play your songs on yet another computer, you have one of two choices: you can deauthorize one of the computers, and then authorize another computer, or you can burn an audio CD and play the songs on the fourth computer using that audio CD.

One issue that can confuse this somewhat is the fact that, technically, you can use more than one Apple ID in your copy of iTunes to buy music. So you may occasionally run across a song in iTunes that won't play because it requires authorization from an Apple ID account that's different from the Apple ID associated with other protected songs in your library.

Fortunately, the solution is straightforward. To find out to whom a particular song is authorized, select it in iTunes and choose File | Get Info. On the Summary tab, look for the entries Purchased By and Apple ID. That tells you who owns the song and what Apple ID login information you would need to authorize (or deauthorize) that song for playback.

command. You should also deauthorize computers before you sell them or give them away to someone who shouldn't have access to your iTunes songs. This is something you can do at any time (even if you haven't reached your three-computer limit), if you simply don't want to be able to play a certain account's songs on a certain computer. (It might also be a good idea to deauthorize your computer before any major maintenance on your Mac's hard disk or, for instance, before reformatting your Mac in order to re-install the operating system.)

You deauthorize a particular computer by going to that computer and choosing Advanced | Deauthorize Computer from the iTunes menu. The Deauthorize Computer dialog box should appear.

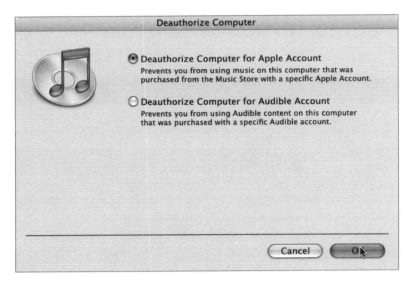

Make your selection (you'll likely choose Apple ID) and click OK. Next, you'll see an Enter Apple ID And Password dialog box—enter the necessary information and click OK. iTunes will attempt to access the Music Store and will report back on whether or not the computer was deauthorized.

If you were successful, but decide you want to authorize this computer after all, that's easily done. Just attempt to play a song that was purchased using the Apple account that you'd like authorized for this computer. When you try to play it, a window will appear telling you that the song is not authorized and asking if you'd like to authorize it. Enter the Apple ID and password for the account associated with this song and click Authorize. iTunes will attempt to connect to the Music Store and confirm that this is allowable, then you'll see a message telling you whether or not it was a success. If it was, you'll now be able to play any music associated with that Apple ID.

Burn a CD

The other way to work with your purchased music is to drag it to a playlist and then burn it to an audio CD. This is perfectly acceptable for purchased songs—otherwise, you wouldn't be able to play your iTunes-bought songs in your car stereo or home audio system. You'll burn purchased music in the exact same way you burn imported songs, as was discussed in Chapter 3.

NOTE   *You'll get an error message if you attempt to burn songs to a CD, and those songs haven't been authorized for playback on your computer. If that happens, you'll need to attempt to play one of the songs in question and then use the dialog box that appears to authorize this computer to play back the protected AAC song(s) you're trying to burn.*

It's interesting to note that burning an audio CD of your purchased songs also gives you a little loophole around the problem of protected AAC files. Once the songs are in audio CD format, they can be played back in any CD player (including a computer's CD player). So, if you have a fourth computer in your house and you don't want to deauthorize your others, you can still play songs from an audio CD that you've burned. (Note that this isn't true for a data CD, as those types of CDs allow the song to maintain its protection. Plus, iTunes won't allow you to create an MP3 CD of purchased Music Store songs.)

How to ... Set Up Allowances and Buy Gift Certificates

Apple is undoubtedly planning to add other features to the iTunes Music Store as ideas and opportunities present themselves. In a recent update during this writing, for instance, the company added the ability for users to buy gift certificates and create *allowances* for other Apple IDs—ideally so that a parent or guardian could give a child a certain amount of credit to work with on the Music Store.

To set up an allowance, find the Allowance link on the Music Store home page—click the small house icon at the top of the main list. (You can also access your Apple ID by clicking it in the Account entry box, and then using the Account Setup screen to add an allowance.) On the screen that appears, you set the amount for the allowance and choose the Apple ID that is to receive it. If you don't have another Apple ID for that user, you can create one; iTunes won't allow you to set up an allowance for your own account. Once the allowance is set up, that user can buy songs using his or her Apple ID without needing a credit card. (To alter or cancel an allowance, access your account setup screen by clicking your Apple ID, and then click Manage Allowances on your Apple Account Information screen.)

Purchasing a gift certificate is similar to setting up an allowance. Click the Gift Certificates link on the Music Store home page and click the Buy button. In the form that appears, enter your name, the recipient's name, and their e-mail address, then choose an amount and send a personal message. You can send a gift certificate to any e-mail address—your recipient will receive an e-mail message complete with a certificate number.

To redeem a gift certificate, click the Redeem Now button in the e-mail you receive from Apple or choose the Gift Certificates link on the Music Store home page and then select the Redeem button. Once redeemed, your Apple ID account is credited with the value of the gift certificate. (Interestingly, it seems that one Apple ID can use a gift certificate that was sent to a different e-mail address—so guard your gift certificates jealously!)

Chapter 5

iTunes for the Dorm Room

How to...

- Check Out Web Radio
- Set Streaming Preferences
- Add Web Radio Stations
- Build Your Own Radio Station
- Use the Visualizer
- Tweak the Equalizer for Better Sound
- Use iTunes with Your Sound System

Okay, so this chapter's title is a little tongue-in-cheek—you don't have to be in a dorm room to use these features. But you can't tell me that the features discussed here—Web radio, streaming MP3, the iTunes music "Visualizer," and its built-in equalizer—wouldn't be popular in the typical dorm room.

Actually, these features can be good for other situations, too. Web radio can be handy for background music as well as for some pretty fascinating explorations into music genres, independent music, and other people's music collections. The Visualizer is just plain fun—definitely something you should set up at an intimate party in your ultra-hip studio apartment (or, even better, an impromptu office party). Meanwhile, we'll round out this chapter with some do-it-yourself advice—how to create your own MP3 radio station, tweak settings in the EQ, and how to hook iTunes up to your home stereo system.

See what I mean about dorm rooms?

Check Out Web Radio

Built into iTunes is the ability to listen to *streaming MP3 audio,* which is simply an MP3 file that is played almost immediately as it arrives over the Internet. While digital music file formats such as AAC and MP3 are good for transferring over the Internet because they're relatively compact, *streaming* technology takes that one step further. With an MP3 stream, the entire file doesn't have to arrive before the song (or other audio) begins playing. Instead, only the first few seconds have to get to iTunes before the digital music file starts playing. Then, the rest of the MP3 is sent across the Internet in a *stream* of data that's played as it arrives in iTunes.

Streaming is popular not only for audio, but for video—you may have used QuickTime, RealMedia, or Windows Media formats that enable you to watch small windows of video almost immediately after launching a channel or video clip over the Internet. MPEG-4 is another popular compression and file format technology for video, as well as for audio. The AAC files used by iTunes are really MPEG-4 AAC files, so, clearly, they stream well over the Internet.

Explore Internet Radio

It so happens that MP3 streams very well, making it the dominant file format for Web "radio" shows. Although the radio we're talking about here has very little to do with the AM/FM type of technology we're accustomed to, it does act somewhat like radio: you can dial in different channels or "stations" and listen to whatever it is that the station is *webcasting*. What these stations are actually doing is offering a steady stream of MP3 data from a server dedicated to the purpose. Your copy of iTunes can elect to connect to that server, receive the MP3 stream, and play it back in iTunes—or, you can move on to the next server and try its stream. Because most of these streams are sent out around the clock, you can usually connect to your favorites anytime you want and listen to whatever has been programmed by the person or people who made that stream happen.

In some ways, this makes Internet radio pretty charming—a great deal of it is non-commercial, amateur, and, often enough, eclectic and interesting. While some Internet radio stations are professionally run—and recently legal challenges and concerns from the music industry have made it a bit more expensive to run an Internet radio station for many of these would-be DJs—a lot of MP3 streams are the labors of love for hobbyists who have a great deal of interest in a particular style or band or artist and are willing to put some work into helping you enjoy the music. There's no question that a lot of the Web radio you'll run into is stuff you won't hear up and down your local AM or FM dial.

Listen to Built-in Radio

iTunes offers a number of stations by default—some of them independent stations, some of them rebroadcasts of on-the-air stations and many of them from Live365.com, a service that enables individuals and organizations to broadcast their own radio stations. To access one of those stations, begin by clicking Radio in the source list. You'll see the main list change to show the different styles of radio stream that are available to you (see Figure 5-1).

5

FIGURE 5-1 When you choose Radio as a source, you'll see a list of genres.

To access a radio station, click the disclosure triangle next to one of the genres and it will open to reveal the stations you can access. When the stations are listed, you'll see the name of the stream, the stream's *bit rate,* and a comment on that stream—usually a description of the "radio station" and its content.

Stream	Bit Rate	Comment
▼ 50s/60s Pop (5 streams)		
🛜 Edgewater Radio	32 kbps	Great Memories from the 50 – 80's
🛜 Industrialinfo	24 kbps	Oldies from Crazy Al's Radio Party, plus te...
🛜 Memory Radio 1	48 kbps	Deutsche Hits aus den 50er, 60er und 70e...
🛜 Memory Radio 2	48 kbps	Deutsche Hits aus den 50er, 60er und 70e...
🛜 Technicolor Web of Sound	56 kbps	95+ hours of no-repeat 60s psych!!!
▶ 70s/80s Pop		
▶ Alt/Modern Rock		
▶ Ambient		

The Stream and Comment columns are probably self-explanatory, but the Bit Rate column holds an interesting entry—it tells you the number of bits per second that the stream will transmit. That translates to a measurement of relative quality—the larger the stream, the better it sounds. However, large streams are only recommended for *broadband* connections (cable, DSL, and other "high-speed" approaches to Internet connectivity). If you have a modem connection to the Internet, you'll want to limit yourself to streams with a bit rate of around 56 kbps or less. For faster connections, you should be able to select any of the streams and enjoy them— the highest bit rates are generally 128 kbps (occasionally, you'll see one higher), which require a good, high-speed connection, but generally won't tax a good broadband modem.

TIP   *The Refresh button in the top-right corner of the iTunes window can be used to check for new stations in your listing, just in case you've had iTunes up and running for a while and want to make sure there aren't more choices.*

Once you've found the stream you want to listen to, double-click it in the list. (You can also select the stream and click the Play button or press the spacebar.) You'll immediately see the small speaker icon appear on the row of that stream, but it may take a few seconds before you'll hear the music in that stream, because iTunes first needs to buffer a little of the music before it will begin playing the stream. (iTunes will allow a few seconds of the stream to arrive before it begins playing so that there are always a few extra seconds stored locally, just in case a very brief glitch occurs in the download process. Often, the buffer is the difference between a smooth-sounding stream and one that is interrupted due to network traffic and has to be renegotiated.)

Occasionally, even with a good buffer (or *often,* if you're listening to a stream that is too large for your Internet connection to handle), you may see a message from iTunes letting you know that the stream has failed and it needs to reconnect.

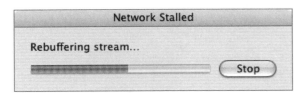

If you see this message more than once within a minute or two—or even more frequently—there's a good chance you're trying to play a stream that is too large for your current Internet connection. You should make sure nothing else is downloaded in the background and, if not, try a smaller stream. (Many Internet radio station streams are fashioned of two types: one that works well for modem connections and one that's of higher quality.) If you know you have a high-speed connection and nothing else is going on in the background on your computer, you might consider restarting the Internet connection just to see if some glitch has been encountered, and if another try at the connection will result in better performance.

The playback controls in the top-left corner can basically be used to stop and start your access to a particular stream—clicking the forward or back button changes the stream you're listening to. You can't pause or stop the stream itself—as with real radio, the songs keep playing even when you aren't listening.

You can add radio streams to your library and to playlists if you want to. Simply click and drag a playlist to your Library icon in the source list, or to an existing playlist on the source list (see Figure 5-2). In fact, you can even drag the radio stream to a blank space on your source list which will prompt a new playlist to be created to hold that one stream. With a stream in a playlist, it's just a little easier to get at. You'll play it the same way, by double-clicking or highlighting it and using the Play button or pressing the spacebar.

FIGURE 5-2   Adding Rockabilly Radio to my playlist of favorite Internet streams

Want to know more about these radio streams? Unfortunately, iTunes doesn't offer songlists for stations or many additional tidbits that might be fun to know. Depending on how the stream has been put together, it may show the title and artist of a song in the Info area. External to iTunes, some Internet streams (although not all) have web sites that tell you a little about the station and what's behind it. It may even show a live playlist. I usually find them by running a search at Google (www.google.com) or a similar service to find the name of the Internet stream. If you hear that the station is part of Live365.com, you can go to www.live365.com to search for it (or search for links to its external page). Sometimes, you'll simply stumble across the station's site (see Figure 5-3).

NOTE   *When you add a stream to your library or to a playlist, that makes it possible for you to select that stream and choose File | Get Info to open the Info window. On the Summary tab, you'll see information about the stream, including the stream's URL. Also, check out the Options tab, where you can choose an equalizer preset or adjust the volume for the stream.*

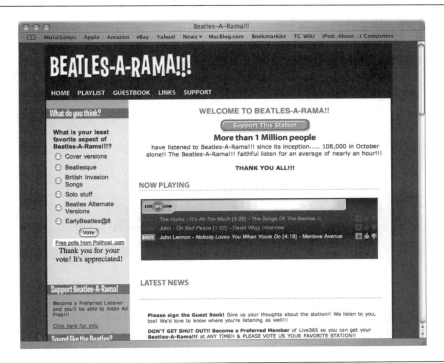

FIGURE 5-3   The web site—complete with scrolling playlist—for Beatles-a-Rama, a Live365-based station I listen to often

Add Other Streams

There are other services that offer streaming MP3 radio stations or feeds, and you'll find that individuals will occasionally have their own servers and streams set up. Usually, all you have to do is click a link to one of these MP3 streams and it will be handled automatically by iTunes. The stream is then added to your library, where you can access it again in the future. In this illustration, for instance, selecting a link to an MP3 stream at the site Digitally Imported (www.di.fm) has automatically added a number of different streams to my iTunes Library; right above that is a stream called Secret Agent that I found at Tastycast (www.tastycast.com). Again, simply clicking a link to the MP3 stream added it automatically to my iTunes Library.

MP3 streams on the Internet will have their own bit rates that you should pay attention to—click a rate that matches your Internet connection (56 kbps or less for a modem connection, higher bit rates for broadband connections). Once these streams are in the iTunes Library, you can add them to playlists, enabling you to gather into one playlist both the built-in Radio streams and any external streams that you add.

NOTE *If iTunes doesn't automatically play the MP3 streams that you select in your web browser, you may not have it set to manage Internet streams. In Mac OS X, choose iTunes | Preferences and make sure the General icon has been selected. Next to the Use iTunes For Internet Music Playback option, click the Set button. In Windows, choose Edit | Preferences, select General, and make sure the option Use iTunes As The Default Player For Audio Files is turned on.*

Deleting a stream works like deleting any song. Simply select the stream in the library and press the DEL key or select Edit | Clear. The representation in your library is really just a handy link to the stream, so when you delete it nothing of substance is deleted. You can return to the web site and click the link to that stream to add it once more.

So where do you go for MP3 streams? You'll find them all over the place, including some of those already mentioned. One of the best places to find online streams is SHOUTCast (www.shoutcast.com), which aggregates link-to streams that are broadcast by amateur DJs. MP3.com (www.mp3.com) is a service that enables you to buy and download MP3s and albums, similar to iTunes Music Store, but the real focus is on gaining exposure for artists. So, you'll find MP3 streams of albums and individual songs, often linked to band and artist pages on the Web. You have to sign in with a name and e-mail address, but you can then listen to streams of entire individual CD cuts from both well-known and independent artists. MP3.com feeds into EMusic (www.emusic.com) for subscription-based access to entire albums in the MP3 format. And, of course, you'll find tons of small bands and hobbyists who offer their own streaming services and webcasts from their web sites. If it's an MP3 stream, it should play back just fine in iTunes.

NOTE   *There are other types of audio streams that you'll encounter. Windows Media is often used for audio streams—the player is built into Windows and is available for Macs at Microsoft's MacTopia (www.microsoft.com/ mactopia/). Real Audio offered the original streaming solution. Although there's an emphasis on video these days, you'll still find tons of audio feeds available via RealNetworks (www.real.com) and elsewhere on the Internet. QuickTime is also a popular technology for streaming, with playback built into the Mac OS and available for Windows (in fact, QuickTime is installed when you install iTunes for Windows). More on QuickTime can be found at www.quicktime.com on the Web. Also, see Chapter 10 for a discussion Mac-specific solutions for recording audio feeds, and for a discussion of Windows Media and Windows-based audio tools.*

How to ... **Build Your Own Station**

Want to do your own broadcasting? There are a few different ways to go about it. It's also worth noting that webcasting has become a bit of a legal minefield these days, so it might behoove you to do a little studying before you begin putting songs on the Web for others to hear. That's particularly true if you intend to put those songs on the Web for profit, although there are caveats for hobbyists as well.

The easiest way to solve all your MP3 streaming issues is to go with a service that provides everything you need. Live365.com is among the most complete solution, in my opinion. Not only does it have tools to help you build your playlists and manage your station, but the service also handles your digital rights issues if you opt to play commercial music. For a hobbyist, you can set up a personal station for (currently) about $8 per month; other packages are available for more professional-level broadcasting.

SHOUTCast enables interested parties to set up a SHOUTCast server and then program that server using Nullsoft WinAmp player, available from Windows. All you do is download the SHOUTCast plug-in and you're able to begin building a playlist for your station. You can install your own server software or locate an ISP that offers SHOUTCast serving as an option. When you build a station, the main SHOUTCast site can be used to promote it and drive listeners to your music. As far as I can tell, SHOUTCast doesn't offer licenses for commercial audio playback, so the legalities are considerably murkier. (As I'm writing this chapter, legal rulings seem to suggest that Internet radio will be held to licensing requirements.) If you've got songs that you've recorded, own, or gained the rights to that you'd like to broadcast (particularly if you also want to set up your own server), then SHOUTCast is a popular solution.

If you are interested in a rights-managed SHOUTCast solution, check out AudioRealm (www.audiorealm.com), which offers streaming server solutions for a variety of formats and also provides a digital rights "umbrella" for broadcasters, allowing you to broadcast commercial music within certain limitations.

The solution that's actually closest to iTunes is QuickTime Streaming Server (QTSS), offered for Mac at www.apple.com/quicktime/products/qtss/ and as an open source option for other platforms at http://developer.apple.com/darwin/projects/streaming/. The streaming server, once installed, enables you to offer MP3 streaming of audio as well as MPEG-4 and QuickTime streaming of video.

I haven't come across any services that manage rights specifically for QTSS solutions, although, regardless of the technology you're using, you can always build your own station and pay for a webcasting license via BMI's digital licensing center (www.bmi.com/licensing/webcaster/index.asp) or ASCAP's new media page (www.ascap.com/weblicense).

Use the Visualizer (...*Dude*)

If anything in iTunes screams "dorm room," it's probably the Visualizer, which is iTune's built-in tech-a-delic ability to create patterns and colors on your screen in step with the beat of the music that's being played via iTunes. The Visualizer works both with digital music files and with Internet radio streams. Once you have some music playing, you can put the Visualizer into motion with a simple click of the mouse.

Turn on Visualizer

To begin, you probably want to be playing some music, although you don't have to be—the Visualizer will work even if there isn't music playing. (It isn't quite as interesting, but it does work.) To turn the Visualizer on, you first select how large you want the Visualizer image to be within the iTunes window by choosing Visualizer | Small, Visualizer | Medium or Visualizer | Large. Then, to turn on the effect, choose Visualizer | Turn Visualizer On or press ⌘-t on a Mac or CTRL-T in Windows. If a song is playing, you'll see an Apple logo, the name of that song, and any artwork associated with it. As the song continues to play, the name and image will disappear and only the Visualizer effect will continue (see Figure 5-4).

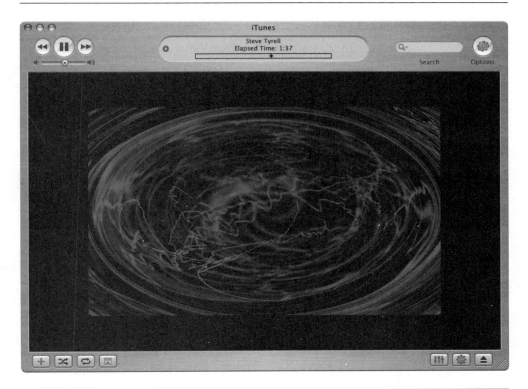

FIGURE 5-4   The Visualizer effect running at Medium size within the iTunes window

*Why choose different sizes? The Visualizer can slow your computer down some, so the smaller the effect, the less of a drag it is on your system while you work on other things.*

While the Visualizer is running, you can access some preferences by clicking the Options button in the top-right corner of the iTunes window. When you do, you'll see a dialog box.

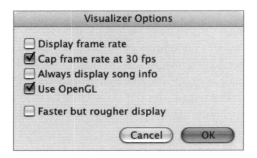

Here's a quick look at the settings:

- **Display frame rate** Turn this option on if you'd like to see the number of frames per second that the Visualizer is able to show onscreen. The Visualizer works to keep the output smooth, and seeing the frame rate can give you a sense of whether it's working too hard given your computer's processor. The lower the frame rate, the more jagged the display (and the more likely it is that your computer is working hard to keep up). You can also press the F key while viewing the Visualizer to toggle this setting.

- **Cap frame rate at 30 fps** Thirty frames per second is the typical speed for North American video and television standards, and it's a good baseline for motion—if the frames per second rate is higher than 30, there's very little benefit to the eye. So, you can cap the framerate, which means iTunes will be less taxing on your processor. Press the T key when viewing the Visualizer to toggle this setting.

- **Always display song info** If you don't want the song's name and artist information to fade away after the first few seconds, turn this option on. Press the I key (for "info") to toggle this setting when viewing the Visualizer.

- **Use OpenGL** This option (only available on Macs) enables you to switch between using Apple's built-in OpenGL technology, which gives iTunes lower-level access to the graphics routines, usually resulting in better performance and crisper graphics.

■ **Faster but rougher display**   If you're having trouble getting a decent frame rate, you can choose this option so that the Visualizer runs smoothly, although the effects might appear more jagged and/or pixilated.

Click OK to close the Visualizer Options dialog box.

The Visualizer offers another option—the ability to watch it full-screen. This can be handy for the aforementioned dorm room and party settings—your computer can sit in and not only play back your favorite songs or Web radio stations, but offer an attractive full-screen display distract your friends and keep them from messing with iTunes or other applications on your computer (and skipping over some of your favorite songs, even if they aren't crowd-pleasers). To enable Visualizer's full-screen mode, choose Visualizer | Full Screen while the Visualizer is being displayed. (If it's not being displayed, select Visualizer | Turn Visualizer On after choosing Full Screen in the menu.) The Visualizer should take over your computer's display with color and patterns. To return to iTunes, press a key or click a mouse button.

NOTE   *Regardless of whether or not the Visualizer is in full-screen mode, you can use the left and right arrow keys to change songs, and use the up and down arrows to change the volume level.*

Customize the Visualizer

The images created by the iTunes Visualizer are made up of a few different components—forms, effects, and colors. iTunes has some keyboard commands you can use to make changes to the Visualizer. The M key (for "mode") can be used to select Freezing Current Config, which stops the Visualizer from randomly changing the patterns so you can experiment with them. You can then use the following keys to make some interesting choices while the Visualizer is displayed:

■ **Q and W**   These keys are used for selecting the forms that the Visualizer employs to represent the waveform of the music. You'll see options such as Radar Sweep, Double-Helix, Spin Doctor, and many, many others.

■ **A and S**   These keys are used to change the effect that the Visualizer uses in the "background" or those that are mixed in with the waveform to create a motion that complements the waveform. The names of these effects are pretty crazy, such as Rolling Hills, Tripping Hard, and Whoo! Whoo!

■ **Z and X**   These keys are used to change the colors that the Visualizer can use. When in randomized mode, you'll see all sorts of colors. But when the mode is frozen, you can pick a particular color scheme, from something simple like Green to selections like Hue Wheel, Volcano, and Sunshine.

- ■ **N**   Use this key to toggle between normal colors and high-contrast colors.

- ■ **SHIFT-*number***   Choose SHIFT and a number (0–9) and you can save the configurations you come up with. You can then press the M key to get into User Config Slideshow mode, which will show your saved settings. Press just the number (0–9) to recall a saved configuration.

Did you get too deep into these changes? You can press the D key to reset everything to the default. Keep in mind, you'll lose your user-saved configurations when you reset to default, so make sure it's really what you want.

Tweak the EQ for Better Sound

No true audiophile (or self-respecting fraternity brother) is going to admit to not understanding the equalizer on a component stereo system. Thankfully, iTunes has a built-in equalizer as well so you can show off your sound-tweaking prowess. But if, like me, you know very little about how to shape sound with an EQ, you can use iTunes' presets to get some surprisingly good sound out of iTunes and your speakers, headphones, or your home stereo system. (See the following "How to" sidebar.)

To view the Equalizer, click the Equalizer button at the bottom-right corner of the iTunes interface (the button with three blue lines) or choose Windows | Equalizer. The Equalizer will appear.

For the EQ to have much of an effect on the music, it needs to be turned on—make sure a check mark is next to the On box. You can then use the pop-up menu to choose from among the many presets available to you. The presets cover all sorts of musical styles, from Pop to Rock to Classical to Hip-Hop. You'll also find some settings for other types of situations, such as Small Speakers, Spoken Word, Bass Booster, or Bass Reducer. If you feel you're in one of those situations, you can choose one of those entries and you'll hear the change within about two beats.

Want to go into manual mode? At any time, you can simply click and drag one of the sliders up and down—the moment you do, the Equalizer goes into Manual mode. Get sliding and dragging until you get things sounding the way you want them. You can then close the Equalizer window by clicking its close control at the top of the window.

If you want to save a manual Equalizer setting, choose Make Preset from the pop-up menu and you'll see a dialog box where you can enter a name for your new entry.

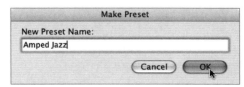

That entry will now appear in the menu.

Do you have a bunch of genres of music in your library? Trying to "ride" the EQ and change it constantly is probably going to seriously hurt your productivity. (Or at least get pretty darned annoying.) The solution is to assign an EQ preset to each individual song so that the EQ will change itself automatically. Choose a song, then choose File | Get Info (press ⌘-I on the Mac or CTRL-I in Windows). In the Info window, choose the Options tab. There you'll see an entry for Equalizer Preset; choose the preset you want to use with this song and then click OK.

TIP   *The settings you make here in the Info window for the Equalizer will carry over to an iPod if you sync your songs with Apple's player.*

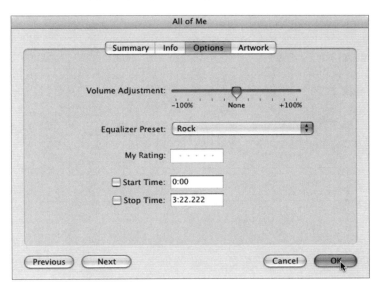

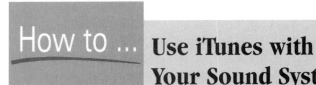

How to ... Use iTunes with Your Sound System

Want to plug your computer into your stereo and play iTunes through some decent speakers? You're not alone. It's a great idea if you don't have high-end computer speakers, or if your computer and your stereo system are convenient to one another and you'd like to use iTunes as if it were another component in your home stereo system. (It could work well for an office system, too, running either Internet radio stations or a constant mix from your iTunes Library. If only my dentist was that cool.)

Treating your computer like a component in your stereo system is exactly what you should try doing. Most desktop computers that have reasonably sophisticated multimedia capabilities have a Line Out port for connecting to audio components. This may be different from a headphone or speaker jack—the line out is designed for connecting to a receiver, usually using a "Y" adapter (in most cases, a *minijack-to-component (RCA-style)* adapter). It'll have a small single connector on one side of the thin cable and two connectors on the other side, which are usually white (left) and red (right) connectors. Those two connectors can be plugged into the back of your receiver. Depending on the receiver, you'll probably want to plug into an AUX input, or perhaps a Video 2 or something that's available on the receiver.

Once that's set up, you can switch the receiver to the AUX or similar input, probably using a dial or button on the front of the receiver. Assuming the stereo is otherwise configured to play through the speakers, you should be able to fire up iTunes and play a song through your stereo. Depending on your receiver and whatever amplifiers you have connected to it, you may want to configure everything in iTunes to a very middle-of-the-road setting. For instance, you may want to turn off the Equalizer, set the volume to a middle range and turn off the Sound Enhancer option in the Effects section of iTunes Preferences. You can then change the volume, Equalizer settings, and other options on your stereo system. (You may also prefer those settings in iTunes, depending on your equipment and how stuffy you are about this sort of thing.)

Chapter 6

iTunes, iPod, and MP3 Players

How to...

- Get the Scoop on iPod
- Sync Your iPod with iTunes
- Sync with Other MP3 Players
- Use Your iPod for Storage
- Use iPod's Contacts and Calendar Features
- Play Your iPod on the Road
- Use iPod Reset and Restore

One way that many iTunes users get their start is by installing it from the CD that came with their iPod. Let's face it, iTunes is a nice little program, but the iPod is the more exciting member of this duo, as it not only allows you to take your song collection away from your computer, but it does so with a level of organization in the process. For example, along with your library of songs, you can also export playlists. Beyond all this, the iPod is handy for other things as well, which we'll touch on in this chapter.

If you have an MP3 (or other compatible type of digital music) player other than an iPod, you may find that it works with iTunes as well. There are tons of digital music players that can be hooked up to your computer and managed by iTunes. And you'll find it's all pretty intuitive.

 *In this chapter, I'll use the name "iPod" to refer to all of the generations of iPod and the iPod mini, in a generic sense, except when I need to refer to a specific model to discuss its features or operation.*

Understand the iPod

I'm fond of saying that the most impressive thing that Apple has done in the iPod is that they've convinced average, everyday people (even some hipsters) to walk around with a hard drive in their pockets. After all, that's exactly what the iPod is—a FireWire (and/or USB 2.0) external, portable hard disk. The electronics for music playback and other interactions are a nice add-on, and, clearly, some clever design ideas and engineering were required to make it compelling. But some of the most amazing capabilities of the iPod come from it being, at its heart, a portable hard disk. And having a hard disk on your person can make for some pretty significant computing advantages.

The most obvious advantage is the sheer storage capacities that iPods are capable of. Even the original iPod, at 5GB, is still something handy to walk around with, and with capacities reaching 40GB and larger, the iPod is, of course, able to store tons and tons of recorded audio in the form of both songs and books. Beyond that, however, the storage capacity means a number of things, such as the ability to store addresses, contacts, documents (by accessing the iPod as a hard disk volume), and, with some of Apple's add-ons, digital photo storage and voice recordings.

At this writing, Apple has had three different "generations" of the iPod, each of which had slightly different features and capabilities. Each generation has come in a variety of capacities, as well. For the most part, any iPod can accomplish the basics we'll talk about in this chapter—they can all synchronize with iTunes and they can handle a large database of digital music. What's different are some of the ancillary issues such as how the iPod connects, the accessories you can connect to the iPod, and so on. Table 6-1 briefly describes the three generations of the iPod.

Which iPod you have doesn't really affect how it works in iTunes—so far, they all work basically the same. The only major difference you'll encounter is the fact that the first and second generations of the iPod don't work with the latest iPod software. As of this writing, iPods that don't have a dock use iPod Software 1.3. Still, it's an important update, as it enables the iPod to work with AAC files and iTunes 4. (To get the update, visit www.apple.com/ipod/download on Apple's web site.)

The latest generation of iPods—and, presumably, those that come after it— have some interesting additional capabilities such as voice recording and storing digital photos, while the first generation iPods are limited to the more mundane, although completely handy, add-ons like contact management and appointment calendar listings. Of course, all iPods are capable of working as external hard disks, which we'll take a look at in this chapter as well.

Generation	Capacities	Characteristics	PC Compatible?
First	5GB, 10GB	Physical scroll wheel, software limited to iPod Software 1.3	Only one PC-compatible model at 5GB
Second	5GB, 10GB, 20GB	Nonmoving scroll wheel, remote control on 10GB and 20GB, also limited to version 1.3 of the iPod Software	All models are PC compatible
Third	10GB, 15GB, 20GB, 30GB, 40GB	New buttons and docking cradle	All models are PC compatible
iPod mini	4GB	Smaller, annodized steel, colors	Yes, and includes USB 2.0 cable and Firewire cable

TABLE 6-1   The iPod Generations

 *Many of the iPod's ancillary capabilities are easier to work with on a Mac than on a PC, although you'll find that there's generally a third-party software solution to mimic most of these capabilities in Windows when they aren't available automatically.*

Get iTunes and Digital Music Players to Work Together

Of course, this book is about iTunes, so we'll begin by talking about how you can use iTunes and your iPod together, and I'll save the fawning over the iPod for later in the chapter. In this section, we'll also take a look at working with other digital music players and iTunes.

Sync Your iPod with iTunes

People who are devoted to iTunes often see the iPod as a portable extension of their iTunes jukebox software. Others view iTunes as music-management software for working with their iPod. Both perspectives are correct. The iPod can work on a number of levels with iTunes. You can integrate an iPod into your well-used iTunes Library and use it to take your iTunes experience "with you," or you can see iTunes as a tool for managing the music that lives with you on a daily basis in your iPod. The only real difference is, probably, how much battery power you end up using.

First-Time Connection

If you've never synchronized your iPod with a computer before—it's either right out of the box or you've recently reset the iPod—then the process is a bit unique. Here's how it works

1. If you haven't yet, launch iTunes.

2. Once it's up and running, connect your iPod to the computer via FireWire or, if the iPod supports it, USB 2.0.

3. The iTunes Setup Assistant will appear, prompting you to make some choices regarding your iPod (see Figure 6-1). Enter a name for your iPod and leave the Automatically Update My iPod option selected if you'd like iTunes to mirror songs from its library to your iPod. (If you turn the option off, you'll place iTunes in a manual mode when updating the iPod, meaning you will have to drag songs back and forth to it to manage its song lists.)

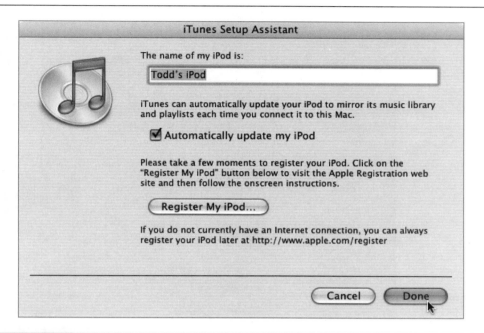

FIGURE 6-1   The iTunes Setup Assistant asks you to enter a name to set up your iPod for the first time.

NOTE   *You can click the Register My iPod button to launch your web browser and fill out Apple's online product registration form.*

When you click Done in the Assistant, you'll switch to the main iTunes window (where you'll see the iPod appear in the source list) and the info area will tell you that the iPod is being updated. (This only happens if you've left the Automatically Update My iPod option selected.) iTunes copies your entire library to the iPod—if it fits—as well as any playlists you've created. You'll need to wait a while for it to happen (see Figure 6-2), but, thanks to the speed of the iPod's connections, it will happen relatively quickly, depending on the size of your library.

NOTE   *What happens if your library won't fit on the iPod? iTunes will switch to a manual mode, so you can choose which songs to copy to it. More on this later in the section "Manual Updating."*

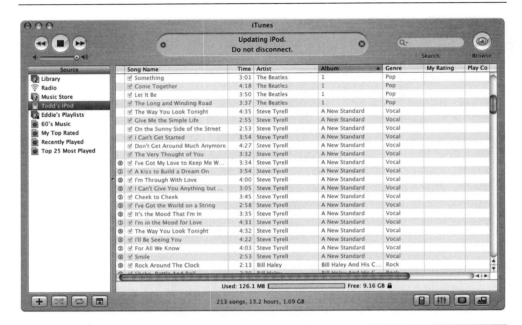

FIGURE 6-2 iTunes updates the iPod by copying all its songs to the iPod.

When the iPod is done updating, you'll be presented with an interesting situation: you'll see the iPod filled with songs, but they'll all be "grayed out" so that you can't access them. When in fully automatic mode, you actually can't access the iPod, even to play the songs on it. This makes sense, because you've presumably just synchronized the iPod and iTunes so that you have the same exact songs. In other words, you don't have any reason to access the iPod.

If you'd prefer to be able to work with the songs on the iPod, you'll just switch to manual mode, as described in the upcoming section "Manual Updating."

Eject iPod

If you're done working with the iPod in iTunes and you want to be able to disconnect it from the computer, choose the iPod in the source list and then select Controls | Eject iPod (you'll actually see the name of the iPod in that command) or simply click the Eject iPod button in the bottom-right corner of the iTunes window.

Automatic Updates

Once you've configured your iPod for the first time and copied your iTunes Library to it, updating it is generally a simple matter—connect the iPod to your computer. That's it. By default, when you connect the iPod to your computer, iTunes will be launched or switched to automatically, and any changes to your library or playlists in iTunes will be noted and synchronized on the iPod.

If you make changes to your Library or playlists after the iPod has synchronized the first time, you can have the iPod updated to reflect those new changes by selecting File | Update Songs on iPod (again, the exact command will have the iPod's name in it).

Auto Update by Playlist

If you want to move out of automatic update mode with your iPod, you have two other choices—you can have the iPod update only certain playlists automatically, or you can move into a fully manual mode, where you update the songs and playlists by dragging songs around in iTunes.

6

> **TIP** *You can create a smart playlist that automatically generates a list of songs and that limits itself to the size of your iPod. For instance, you could turn off the Match the Following Condition criterion and turn on the Limit criterion in Smart Playlist, creating a criterion line something like* `Limit to 30GB` *selected by* `Random` *if you'd like iTunes to keep you guessing with what it puts on your iPod. See Chapter 2 if this smart playlist stuff doesn't make sense to you yet or if you want so more ideas for smart playlists.*

The magic of how you make these changes is hidden in the iPod Preferences, which you get to by first selecting your iPod in the source list and then clicking the iPod Preferences icon in the lower-right corner of the iTunes window.

When you do that, you'll see the iPod Preferences window, which is shown in Figure 6-3. As you can see in the figure, you switch modes by selecting one of the radio buttons—in this case, the Automatically Update Selected Playlists Only. You then select the playlists that you'd like to keep synchronized between iTunes and the iPod. When you've made those decisions, click OK in the dialog box and they'll be implemented (immediately, in fact) by iTunes.

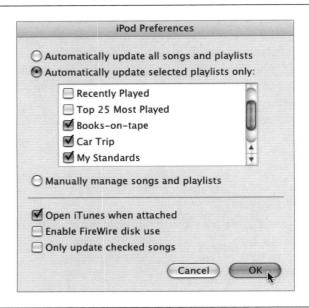

FIGURE 6-3   The iPod Preferences window is used to set how iTunes will update
your iPod.

Updating by playlist can be particularly handy if you use iPod only under
certain circumstances—such as in the car, when you're working out, or if you
want to limit the amount of space your songs take up on the iPod, but want a
"semi-automatic" solution where you don't have to drag items from your library
to the iPod. Simply update your playlists in iTunes whenever you get the desire
and then connect the iPod to the computer. If iTunes is still in this semi-automatic
mode, it will update the playlists when you connect and whenever you subsequently
choose File | Update Songs On iPod.

*The iPod Preferences dialog box includes an Only Update Checked Songs
option, which can be used to limit the songs that iTunes synchronizes with
your iPod when it's set to an automatic mode. Turn on this option and then
click to remove the check mark next to songs in your Library that you don't
want synchronized to your iPod.*

Manual Updating

The last option enables you to manage your iPod by simply placing the songs on
it you want and leaving off the songs you don't—simple enough, right? It can,
however, be a bit of work when you've got tons of songs in your library. But, hey,
it's your free time.

To turn on manual mode, launch the iPod Preferences window and click the radio button next to Manually Manage Songs and Playlists.

When you click this option, you'll see a dialog box that reminds you that you'll need to manually unmount the iDisk (eject it in iTunes) before disconnecting it. One of the advantages of the automatic modes is that you can disconnect your iPod at any point after the automatic synchronizing has happened. In manual mode, you'll need to eject the iPod by clicking the Eject iPod button in the bottom-right corner or by selecting the iPod in the source list and selecting Controls | Eject iPod.

When you move into manual mode, you're able to see and access all of the songs on your iPod, as shown in Figure 6-4. You can manage the list just as you would any playlist (or even the library) that appears in the source list.

To add songs to the iPod, switch to your library and drag the songs to the iPod's entry on the source list, just as you would if you were adding songs to a playlist. The only real difference is the fact that the songs you drag to the iPod are actually copied to the iPod, so you'll see that progress in the information area at the top of the iPod window. (It usually doesn't take too long thanks to the speed of FireWire or USB 2.0.)

As you may know from working with your iPod, you can have playlists on the iPod that you can use the same way you use them in iTunes: to organize your songs and limit playback to certain songs in whatever manner you've grouped them. To add a playlist to your iPod while you're working in manual mode, make sure the

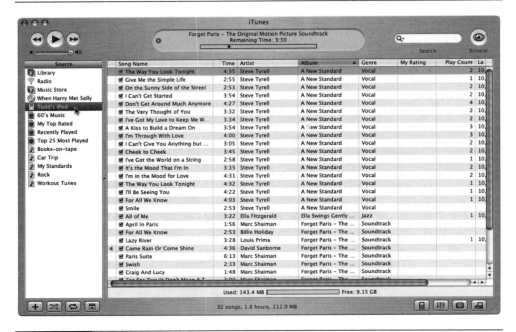

FIGURE 6-4 When you switch to manual mode with your iPod, it becomes an active item in the source list.

iPod is selected in the source list and then choose File | New Playlist. You'll see an untitled playlist appear, enabling you to immediately edit the name.

Give the playlist a name and then press RETURN. Now you can drag songs either from the iPod's own library or from your iTunes Library to that playlist. When you drag the songs from the iTunes Library, they'll be copied to the iPod if they aren't already there, and be added to the playlist.

You can also add playlists by dragging them from your source list to the iPod. When you drop an existing playlist on the iPod, it will be added to the iPod's playlists (as well as be included in the source list), and any songs on that list that aren't already on the iPod will be placed there.

You can add as many playlists as you like in the same way and, as with iTunes, you can use the same song in multiple playlists if you like. They're simply there for your organizing benefit—and they're certainly handy on the iPod.

iPod Info

Wondering how much space you've got on your iPod? It's a little more important to know when you're in manual mode, but it's interesting in any mode. iTunes shows you right at the bottom of the display when your iPod is selected.

| Used: 618.6 MB | Free: 8.68 GB |

Your iPod and Other Computers with iTunes

When you sync your iPod to your computer, that computer becomes the default for that iPod. If you subsequently attach that iPod to another computer running iTunes, your results will be interesting. If that copy of iTunes is set to automatically update an iPod, then you'll see a dialog box asking you if you want to replace all the songs on your iPod with the songs in this iTunes Library. You probably don't want to do that, but if you do, click OK. Otherwise, click No.

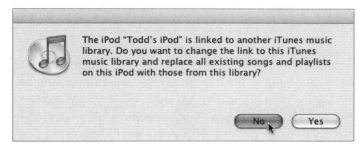

The iPod "Todd's iPod" is linked to another iTunes music library. Do you want to change the link to this iTunes music library and replace all existing songs and playlists on this iPod with those from this library?

No   Yes

In order to work with an iPod that's connected to another copy of iTunes, it's best to be in manual mode. Open iPod preferences and select Manually Manage Songs and Playlists. That will enable you to do two things—first, you'll be able to add songs to that iPod from the iTunes Library. Second, you'll be able to playback songs directly from the iPod from within that copy of iTunes. Note that what you *can't* do is copy songs from your iPod to that second copy of iTunes—that's one way that Apple tries to limit piracy of copyrighted songs. But, it's also why it can be handy to play songs directly from the iPod. If you've got "Paperback Writer" by the Beatles on your iPod and you want to play it back using this secondary copy of iTunes, you can't drag the song to the library to add it, but you can play it back directly off the iPod (see Figure 6-5).

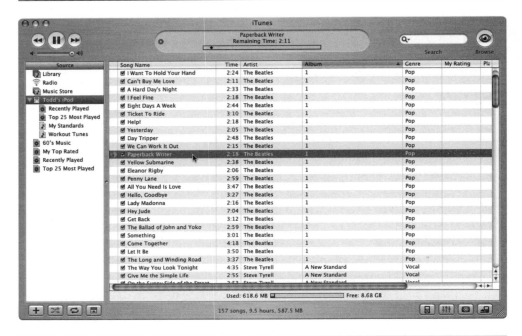

FIGURE 6-5   Me playing a song off my iPod in a different copy of iTunes

Sync with Other Digital Music Players

You don't *have* to have an iPod if you want to take your iTunes songs with you—it's just that the iPod (subjectively speaking) is the *coolest* way to go. There are plenty of other choices and a fair number of them are compatible with iTunes. If you do opt for a third-party player, check for iTunes compatibility on the box or in that device's documentation.

To get started, plug the device into your Mac or PC and see if it comes up in the source list of iTunes. If it does, then it should be compatible. Now, you can drag and drop songs to add them to the device—unlike an iPod, most don't support iTune's playlists, although you may be able to arrange the songs on the device the way you want them (see Figure 6-6).

One thing to watch out for is that some third-party MP3 players aren't AAC compatible, which might be the format that you're using for the songs you're importing from CDs, and it's the song format that Apple uses to sell songs from the iTunes Music Store. For the songs that you've imported, you might want to translate them to MP3 first. You can do that by selecting the song in your library

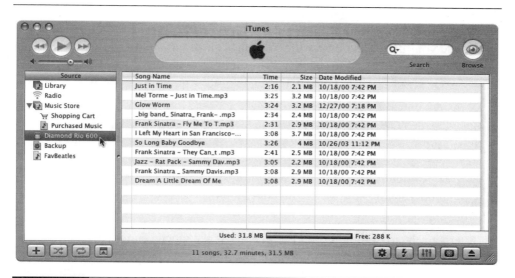

FIGURE 6-6   Updating a third-party MP3 player

and choosing Advanced | Convert Selection To MP3. (If that option doesn't say MP3, then launch iTunes Preferences, click the Importing button and choose MP3 Encoder from the Import Using menu. Click OK and the command in the Advanced menu will now say Convert Selection To MP3.) This conversion won't work for songs that you bought from the Music Store or any other protected songs.

 *See Chapter 9 for more on translating and converting files between the various formats.*

More with the iPod

Before we move on to discussing other MP3 players and iTunes, let's take a slight detour and look at the iPod itself, including some behaviors you control from iTunes, as well as some other applications that you might consider using with your iPod in conjunction with your iPod and iTunes.

Use Your iPod for Storage

In the iPod Preferences dialog box, you can choose to Enable FireWire Disk Use when you have updating set to an automatic mode. What that does is mount the iDisk on your desktop, which lets you access it as if it were a typical external hard disk. You can't actually manipulate digital music that way since digital music files are hidden in the Finder or Windows Explorer. The FireWire disk option allows you to use your iPod as an external hard disk. You can drag any sort of file or folder to the iPod, using it for backup or for transferring to other computers (see Figure 6-7). This is great if you use different computers in the office and at home, or even if you want to move from computer to computer within an organization and have your important files with you at all times. (You can see why I think it's brilliant that Apple used the iPod to convince people to walk around with a portable hard disk.)

 *The Enable FireWire Disk Use option is not available when you're in a manual mode with iTunes because manual mode, by definition, mounts the iPod as a hard disk.*

Another related option in iPod Preferences is the Open iTunes When Attached option. If you turn this option off, then connecting your iPod to your computer will simply mount it on the desktop so you can use it primarily as an external hard disk.

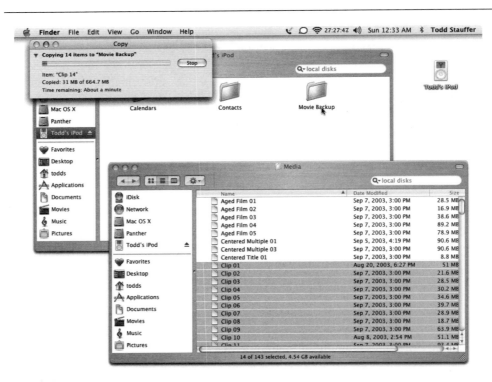

FIGURE 6-7   Me copying files from my hard disk to a folder on my iPod in order to (in this example) have them stored for backup purposes.

Then, if you want to play back or manage songs, you can manually launch iTunes and let it do its magic. (Or you can manually do this magic on your own, according to your preferences.)

The iPod can be used for storage on a PC as well since the Windows version of the iPod is formatted as a Windows disk. Simply connect and, if you've chosen to mount the iPod as a disk in iPod Preferences, you'll see the iPod appear as an available disk when you double-click My Computer (see Figure 6-8). You can access it as you would any disk. To eject it, right-click the iPod icon and choose Eject.

NOTE   *Of course, an iPod in Windows isn't necessarily a FireWire disk since you can use USB 2.0 to connect some iPod models in Windows. So, it's simply an external disk, as the command in the iPod Preferences of Windows' version of iTunes suggests.*

Other iPod Applications

Another thing that Apple continues to do with the iPod is come up with ways for the device—even with its limited computing ability and relatively small LCD display—to be useful for storing other types of data. For instance, using Apple's iSync software, you can store contact information from Apple's Address Book and

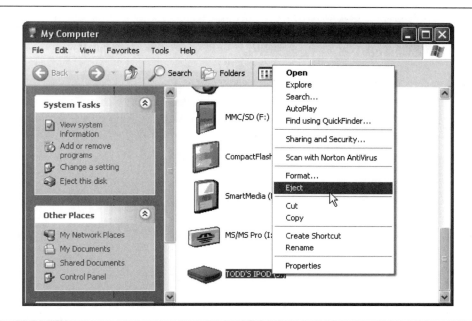

FIGURE 6-8   Using an iPod in Windows as an external disk

also synchronize events from your software with that of your iCal software. This way, you're able to access that information using nothing more than the scroll control and buttons on your iPod. You'll find a special menu on the iPod's display screen, called Extras, that gives you access to your contact and calendar information.

On a Windows PC or a machine running Linux or Unix, iSync isn't an option, but a number of third-party tools are available to fill the gap.

iSync

To use iSync, launch it from the Applications folder in Mac OS X. If your iPod is connected, you'll see it appear in iSync window. Select it and the iSync window opens up to reveal options for controlling its behavior (see Figure 6-9). Make your choices as to the type of contacts and calendars you'd like to sync (both Address Book and iCal enable you to organize your people and events in various categories such as personal, business, and so on). When you're done making choices, click the Sync Now button and iSync will go to work.

> **NOTE** *The iSync window gives you two other important options to consider: Turn On iPod Synchronization and Automatically Synchronize When iPod Is Connected. The first option is used to turn off synchronization. iSync is designed to perform all of its device synchronizations at once, so if, at some point, you want to stop synchronizing with the iPod by not removing it as a device, then just turn off that option. The second option can be handy, too, since it will automatically synchronize your iPod with Mac OS X's Address Book and iCal whenever you plug in your iPod.*

iSync isn't the only solution—you can actually perform this synchronization manually. After all, what is really happening here is that special files are being placed in folders on the iPod that you can access by mounting the iPod as a FireWire disk.

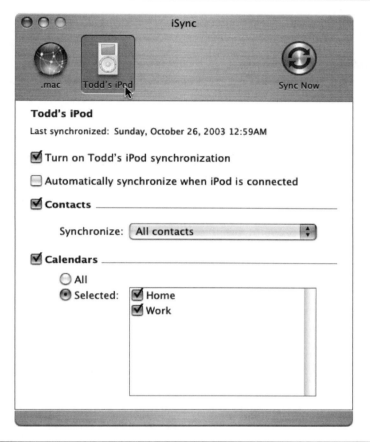

FIGURE 6-9   The iSync window opens to reveal iPod synchronization options.

To add to your contacts, you can copy any vCard (.vcd) files into the Contacts folder on the iPod and they'll show up as contacts in the iPod's Extras menu. (And, you'll be able to synchronize them with Address Book or other compatible contact databases.) vCard is the standard format for contact information. These days, more and more people are attaching personal vCard files to their e-mails so you can easily add their contact information to your contact manager.

Calendars are stored in ICS (.ics) format, which is also a standard format that can be shared between various applications and platforms. The advantage of synchronizing your calendar to the iPod is two-fold—you can carry it with you to consult events and contacts, and you can use the iPod to synchronize two different computers (one at work and one at home, for instance).

Other Mac Software

While iTunes is certainly the dominant software on the Mac platform—and iSync comes with the Mac OS, so there isn't much point in duplicating its functions—there is some third-party software available for the Mac and iPod. Applications such as PodWorks (www.scifihifi.com/podworks) and iPod Rip (www.thelittleappfactory .com/software/ipodrip.php) are designed to enable you to copy songs from your iPod to your Mac and to give you an alternative to iTunes for synchronization.

Other applications are even more fun, such as PodMail (www.podmail.org) that allows you to download e-mail messages from your Mac to your iPod so you can read your e-mail on the iPod's screen or keep important messages with you. (It's specifically designed for .Mac members at this writing, but future support for other types of accounts may happen in the future.)

iPod It (www.zapptek.com/ipod-it) is designed to synchronize Entourage, Stickies, mail messages, Address Book, and iCal content to your iPod, along with weather forecasts and news headlines from the Web. iSpeak It (www.zapptek.com/ispeak-it) can "read" a text file into an audio file that can be stored in the iTunes Library and played back on an iPod. This is great for listening to documents that you don't have time to read, or even for creating your own audio books from public-domain classics that you can download off the Internet.

You'll find that applications with a primary focus on desktop tools (such as Chronos' Personal Organizer) also have the ability to synchronize contact information and additional types with an iPod using vCard and other standards.

Windows and Linux Options

As far as Apple is concerned, the iPod, when used with Windows or Unix, is mostly a music machine, although it can easily be used as an external drive on those platforms as well, and can display contact information that's added using vCards as well as standard calendar information in .ics format. But what if you'd prefer a full-fledged application for managing your iPod's "other" features from Windows or Linux?

You've definitely got some options. Red Chair Software makes Anapod Explorer (www.redchairsoftware.com/anapod), an iTunes replacement that can do some amazing things, such as making your iPod's contents available via a web browser or translating them between file formats. The point of the software is to make working with your iPod a more "integrated Windows experience," meaning you can access your iPod directly from the My Computer icon and use right-click menus and so on to synchronize and manage your songs.

Xplay from Mediafour (www.mediafour.com/xplay) is software for Windows that enables you to use a Mac-formatted iPod with Windows, enabling you to switch back and forth between the two platforms. (If you use your iPod exclusively with Windows, then you probably don't need Xplay since its major claim to fame is Mac-to-Windows translation.) Xplay lets you access the iPod as a hard disk, add items to the Contacts database, and, of course, manage your music.

iPodSync (iccnet.50megs.com/iPodSync) is software that enables you to synchronize data in Microsoft Outlook with your iPod, including contacts, calendars, tasks, and even weather forecasts and news from the Web. It can work with Xplay for a Mac-formatted iPod or on its own with a Windows-formatted iPod—the trick is that the iPod has to appear in Windows with a drive letter.

For Linux and similar platforms, GNUPod (www.gnu.org/software/gnupod) is actually a collection of Perl scripts that can be used in your iPod with Linux. EphPod is another popular choice (www.ephpod.com) that's designed for synchronization under either Windows or Linux. It can also download eBooks, weather, and other web-based information for review within the iPod. There's even a Java-based, platform-independent interface for the iPod, called MyPod (mypod.sourceforge.com) that lets you create and synchronize playlists on an iPod or any platform where you can get the iPod mounted.

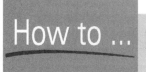

How to ... **Play Your iPod in the Car**

One key concern for many iPod owners is figuring out how to use your iPod in your car. After all, a car is where a lot of us spend most of our quality music-listening time, and it's nice to be able to use your iPod instead of commercial radio, for instance.

You've got a couple of approaches. If you have a cassette player in your car, consider yourself lucky (since cassettes seem like old technology.) With a cassette adapter—a fake cassette that includes wires which can plug into your iPod—you can listen to your iPod easily through you car stereo. These adapters can vary somewhat in quality, so buy a nicer one if you can. Thankfully, even the nicer ones are relatively inexpensive.

If a cassette adapter doesn't make sense or isn't an option for you—or if you'd like to use your iPod in multiple locations—the solution may be an FM transmitter. A number of different transmitter kits have been designed specifically for the iPod. The transmitter itself emits a very low-range FM signal—usually ten feet or less—that can be targeted at an unused FM radio frequency. That way, you're able to listen to your iPod through your stereo, hopefully with a minimum of interference or static. Some kits aimed specifically at the iPod are made by Dr. Bott (www.drbott.com) and Griffin Technologies (www.griffintechnology.com).

iPod Troubleshooting

We'll cover three quick troubleshooting items in this section, each of which you may find helpful in dealing with your iPod. They include updating your iPod's software, resetting your iPod, and restoring it to its original state.

Update Your iPod

Periodically, Apple releases new software for the iPod that you can use for updating it. On the Mac, this software comes in the form of the iPod Software Updater, which can be obtained from Apple's Support site or, in some cases, downloaded using the Software Update feature in Mac OS X. Once you have the Software Updater downloaded and installed, you can launch it while your iPod is attached to your Mac (see Figure 6-10).

 *The software updater you need may depend on the iPod you have—first and second generation iPods require different software from the more recent dock-based iPod models.*

To update the iPod, first click the padlock tools and enter a username and password for an administrative user. Next, click the Update button in the window. If the button is grayed out and can't be selected, that's because the software on the iPod is already up-to-date.

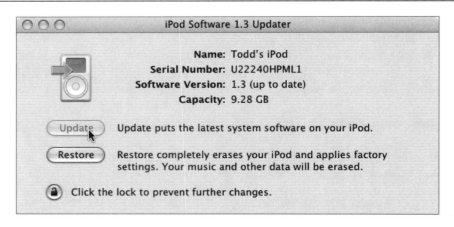

FIGURE 6-10   The iPod Updater software for Mac

Apple also makes an iPod Updater for Windows, which has the same basic functions. You can launch the updater to either update the iPod or restore it. When you restore your iPod using the Windows version of the updater, you, of course, restore it to the Windows format and its various compatibilities.

Reset Your iPod

There are two ways to reset the iPod: a "soft" reset and a full restore of the iPod to its original factory condition. In the first case, you're really just clearing current memory and sending the iPod through its startup process again. This can be useful if you're having odd problems such as an iPod that won't wake from sleep or that skips when playing back songs. For a soft reset, do the following:

1. Either plug in the iPod using its power adapter or connect to a FireWire cable that's connected to a powered FireWire port.

2. Click the Hold switch on the top of the iPod from off to on, and back again to off.

3. Press and hold down both the Play button and the Menu button on the iPod until the Apple logo appears.

Now, wait for the Apple logo to disappear and the iPod's menus to return. You should still retain any songs, contacts, and other items stored in the iPod. On some iPods, however, you'll lose information in your smart playlists such as "on-the-go" playlists.

To restore your iPod, simply launch the iPod Software Utility, authenticate with an administrator's username and password (in the Mac version; this isn't necessary in Windows) and then click the Restore button. You'll be asked to confirm your decision—click Restore again if you're sure this is what you want to do.

The iPod will be erased and its preferences restored to the factory defaults. The next time you launch iTunes and connect your iPod, you'll be greeted with the iPod Assistant dialog box asking you to name the iPod.

TIP

The Restore feature can be used to change the format of an iPod as well. If you have a Windows-formatted iPod that you'd like to transform into a Mac-formatted iPod, simply connect it to the Mac and run the iPod Software Updater appropriate for that iPod version. Use the Restore feature on the iPod and it will be restored to a Mac-compatible factory setting. Afterward, you can use it with iTunes, the Finder, iSync, and other native Mac applications.

Chapter 7

Become an iTunes Expert

How to...

- Use Keyboard Commands and Quick Maneuvers
- Use Rendezvous and iTunes Library Sharing
- Use iTunes' Preference Settings

Okay, you've got the basics, now you're ready to dig in and learn how to become an iTunes power user, right? Actually, there's not *that* much to it. iTunes is a pretty simple application, and there aren't a whole lot of hidden features. That doesn't mean there isn't some hidden power, however, so we'll use this chapter to take a look at some different tips and tricks, as well as discuss in depth the iTunes preference settings and iTunes' built-in ability to share libraries among networked computers.

Keyboard Commands and Quick Maneuvers

iTunes is one of those computer applications that you're likely to leave running constantly in the background when you're working on your computer, since you'll be switching back and forth to it often. After all, if you're managing all of your digital music in iTunes, you might launch it and work with it almost daily. So, for any program that you'll be spending this much time with, getting to know its shortcuts is a good idea.

iTunes has tons of keyboard commands that are worth knowing. You've been introduced to a few already in previous chapters, but this chapter will gather them all together and discuss some new ones as well. We'll begin with a look at keyboard commands that you can use for various situations. Then, we'll discuss some tips for getting things accomplished a bit faster.

Keyboard Commands

One way to move around the iTunes interface more quickly is to get accustomed to the keyboard commands, which can be used for everything from playback to creating new playlists to turning on the Visualizer. Not everything in iTunes can be accomplished with just the keyboard—which is probably a good thing, because some things are simply better managed with a mouse. But the keyboard does enable you to move around more quickly and accomplish many tasks more efficiently. It's also worth noting that some keyboard commands are actually something we could call keyboard *modifiers*—they work with a mouse-click to modify that mouse-click's behavior.

We'll start with the keyboard commands for playback (see Table 7-1). These are commands you can use when you have an item highlighted in the main list or when viewing a playlist or playing back songs on an iPod or similar device.

The next set of keyboard commands and keyboard modifiers are those that you use when dealing with the library or playlists, whether you're reorganizing, adding songs to the lists, or removing them. Some of these modifiers you'll want to use in combination with a mouse movement, so that's been added to Table 7-2 as well.

As you can see, there's tons of stuff you can do with the keyboard when you're managing items in lists. iTunes also enables you to use the standard Cut (⌘-x or CTRL-X, in Mac and Windows, respectively), Copy (⌘-c; CTRL-C), and Paste (⌘-v; CTRL-V) to copy and paste text when it's highlighted in a song's name, the Info window, and so on.

Finally, iTunes has a number of keyboard shortcuts you can use to accomplish things in the interface, shown in Table 7-3.

7

Mac Combination	Windows Combination	What It Does...
Spacebar	Spacebar	Play the current song
Up Arrow	Up Arrow	Highlight previous song
Down Arrow	Down Arrow	Highlight next song
Left Arrow	Left Arrow	Return to beginning of song (goes to previous song with the first few seconds of a song)
⌘+RightArrow	Control+Right Arrow	Play next song if iTunes is currently playing music
⌘+Left Arrow	Control+Left Arrow	Play previous song if iTunes is currently playing music
⌘+Up Arrow	Control+Up Arrow	Volume up
⌘+Down Arrow	Control+Down Arrow	Volume down
⌘+Option+Down Arrow	Control+Alt+Down Arrow	Mute song as it plays
⌘+Left Arrow	Control+Shift+Left Arrow	Previous chapter (in an audiobook)
⌘+Shift+Right Arrow	Control+Shift+Right Arrow	Next chapter (in an audiobook)
Option+Left Arrow	Shift+Control+Alt+Left Arrow	Move to previous album
Option+Right Arrow	Shift+Control+Alt+Right Arrow	Move to next album

TABLE 7-1 Playback Keyboard Controls

Mac Combination	Windows Combination	Mouse Movements	What It Does...
Shift+arrow keys	Shift+arrow keys	N/A	Highlight contiguous songs
Up and Down Arrow keys	Up and Down Arrow keys	N/A	Move between songs in a list
Shift	Shift	...then click add (+) button	Create a playlist from highlighted songs
⌘-n	CTRL-SHIFT-N	N/A	Create a playlist from highlighted songs
⌘+N	Control+N	N/A	Create a new (empty) playlist
Shift+⌘+N	Control+Alt+N	N/A	Create a smart playlist
⌘+O	Control+O	N/A	Add a new song to the library
Shift+⌘+O	Shift+Control+O	N/A	Import a song or playlist
⌘+I	Control+I	...after selecting a song	Get information about a song
⌘+R	Control+R	...after selecting a song	Show a song's file in the Finder or Explorer
⌘+Delete	Control+Delete	N/A	Delete a playlist without a confirmation dialog box
Option+Delete	Shift+Delete	...after selecting a playlist with the mouse	Delete a playlist and remove the songs in that playlist from the library
Option+Delete	Shift+Delete	...after selecting a song in the library	Delete highlighted songs in the library from both the library and from any playlists

TABLE 7-2   Keyboard Combinations and Modifiers for Managing iTunes Lists

Learn the Shortcuts

When you're importing songs from audio CDs, iTunes makes it easy to import an entire CD but a little more difficult to import individual songs from the CD, because you have to deselect the tracks you don't want. To save time, there's another option you can use. Instead of unchecking the songs you don't want, simply highlight the song or songs you want to import, then choose Advanced | Convert Selection To AAC or Advanced | Convert Selection The MP3. (The exact command depends on your current setting on the Importing screen of iTunes Preferences.)

Mac Command	Windows Command	What It Does...
⌘+M	Windows Key	Minimize the window
⌘+1	N/A	View the iTunes window
⌘+2	N/A	View the EQ window
⌘+?	F1	View Help
⌘+T	Control+T	Toggle the Visualizer on and off
⌘+F	Control+F	While Visualizer is running, make it Full Screen
⌘+U	Control+U	Open a URL window so you can enter the specific address of an MP3 stream
⌘+K	N/A	Connect to shared libraries or playlists over a network
⌘+E	Control+E	Eject the CD or MP3 player/device
⌘+B	Control+B	Toggle the display of the Artist and Album columns in the iTunes window
⌘+G	Control+G	Toggle the display of artwork
⌘+J	Control+J	Open the View preferences for the list you're viewing
⌘+W	Alt+F4	Close the iTunes window

TABLE 7-3   iTunes keyboard shortcuts for use in the Interface

If you do want to work with the checked list, remember that ⌘+clicking a checkbox will toggle all of the checkboxes on or off. So, you could, for instance, toggle off all of the checkboxes for a particular CD, then toggle on only the checkboxes for the songs you want to import, then click the Import button in the iTunes window, if that's the way you like to do it.

⌘+clicking or CTRL-clicking works under another interesting circumstance—when you click the disclosure triangle for a genre of Radio stations. If you hold down the modifier key, you'll open *all* of the genre's disclosure triangles (see Figure 7-1); hold and click again, and you'll close them all.

Another fun workaround enables you to quickly create a playlist by simply selecting a number of songs (remember that you can use the ~ CM key on a Mac or the CTRL key in Windows to select multiple, noncontiguous songs) and dragging them from the library to a blank spot on the Source menu. When you drop the songs, a playlist will be created instantly (see Figure 7-2).

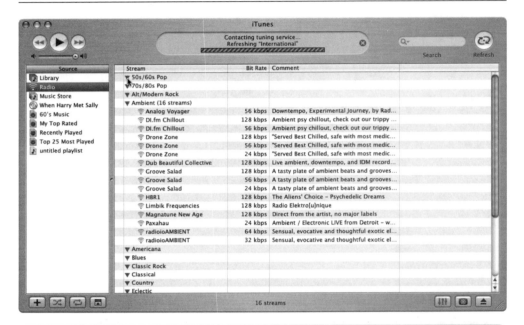

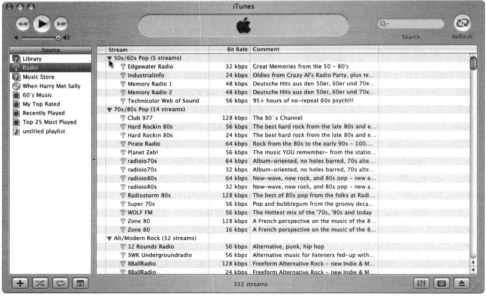

FIGURE 7-1   Using a modifier key (top), you can quickly open and close all of the Radio genres (bottom).

FIGURE 7-2   Dragging and dropping songs on the source list (top) will create a playlist of those songs automatically (bottom).

Having trouble seeing everything in the iTunes window? Hold down the OPTION key and click the Maximize button at the top of the iTunes window. (Buttons are on the top-left in the Mac version and on the top-right in Windows.) Doing so should give you an "optimally" sized screen (so that the most text possible can fit).

As was mentioned in Chapter 1, if you simply click the Maximize button without a modifier key, you'll find that something very interesting happens—your iTunes screen minimizes to a tiny window that's useful for basic playback only:

What we didn't cover in Chapter 1 about this little window is that you can actually click and drag on the bottom-right corner of it. Drag all the way to the right and you'll expand the information portion of this window so you can see more information about the song, book, or station you're listening to.

Slide the window all the way to the left and you'll see the information area disappear completely leaving only the bare minimum of controller area.

Rendezvous and iTunes Library Sharing

Easily one of the coolest features in iTunes is the music-sharing feature that uses Apple's Rendezvous (also called "ZeroConf") technology. What Rendezvous does is allow network devices and software to be automatically located on a local TCP/IP network. Instead of requiring you to plug in the exact address of a printer or scanner, for instance, Rendezvous technology allows your computer to find the device on its own.

With iTunes's built-in Rendezvous implementation, it becomes possible for one copy of iTunes to share its library or certain playlists with other copies of iTunes on other computers connected to your network. In other words, you can make all or some of your songs available to other people in your office, organization, or home (wherever this particular computer is), simply by flipping a switch in the iTunes Preferences window.

What makes this work is not just Rendezvous, but the fact that iTunes has built in a mini MP3 streaming radio server of sorts. It's able to stream songs over the network connection to the iTunes applications that are ready and able to receive it. What you've got is a sort of mini radio station built into iTunes that's able to make its playlist available to other computers on your LAN. Those computers can even play the same song at the same time.

NOTE   *If you're familiar with iTunes 4.0, you may notice that in later versions, Apple has pared back the song sharing capabilities; originally, you could share music on the Internet, but Apple now limits you to a local network. (Technically, you're limited to the same subnet mask, which is meaningful to you if you know something about TCP/IP networking.)*

Share Your Songs

So how do you flip that switch? In the Mac version, choose iTunes | Preferences; in the Windows version, choose Edit | Preferences. Now, in the iTunes Preferences window, click the Sharing icon. To share your music with others, click the checkbox next to the Share My Music option (see Figure 7-3).

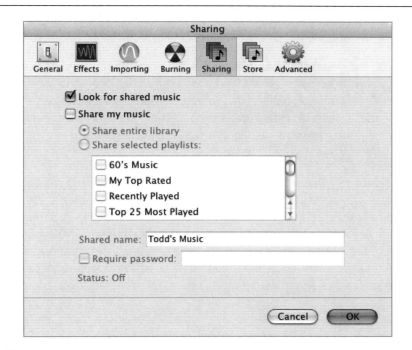

FIGURE 7-3   The Sharing controls in the iTunes Preferences window

Share Entire Library

Once sharing is active, you have some choices to make. If you'd like, you can share your entire library with others or you can create playlists that you share across the network. The advantage of sharing your library is that you don't have to do much preparation—simply click the Share Entire Library radio button control.

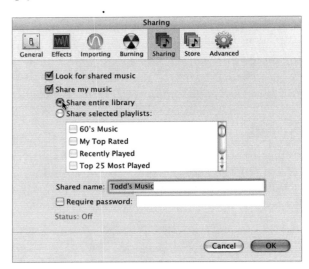

Click OK and your library will be available in any other copies of iTunes that are properly configured on a network connection and that are set to look for shared music. The only real caveat to this is that a computer that isn't authorized for protected songs (those that have been bought on the Apple Store) can't play those songs without first authorizing the computer in question. That requires entering an Apple ID and password, as was discussed in Chapter 4.

NOTE   *Remember, you can only authorize three computers using your Apple ID, which allows those computers to play songs bought from the Apple Store using your Apple ID. If you want to allow someone else's computer on your network to play songs you've bought in the iTunes Music Store, that computer must be one of the three. And if you've already authorized three computers, you'll need to deauthorize one before anyone else can play a bought song (even if it's shared, as we're discussing here).*

Share Playlists

You can also opt to share individual playlists with others. This takes more preparation, but it makes playback a bit more convenient for those with whom you're sharing. If you have a large library, then sharing it makes finding songs a bit tougher on the people with whom you're sharing, because iTunes won't let you rearrange a shared library. You can't drag items out of a shared library or even arrange them in a playlist. So, if you set up the playlists on your side, it makes things a bit easier for the people who are the recipients of your sharing kindness.

Plus, building playlists enables you to limit the songs you share with others. You can keep out the songs you've bought from the Music Store, for instance, particularly if you don't want those people calling you to ask why they can't listen to those songs. (Hey, some of us are the computer people in our groups or families, and others aren't. There's nothing wrong with that.) And, building playlists also lets you limit what you share out of your library for other reasons—maybe you don't want your sharing recipients to know about your extensive Barry Manilow, Yanni, or Weird Al Yankovic collections. (All three artists, by the way, have sold huge numbers of records, so there's no point in pretending that no one is out there buying their stuff. I'll let you guess which of the three I keep in my library.)

NOTE *When you share your entire library, all of your playlists are also shared. Just something you should know, in case any of them have embarrassing names ("Showtunes I Sing to My Plants," for instance).*

To share playlists, first create them as discussed in Chapter 2. Once you've put together the playlists you want to share with others, you turn on the Share My Music option, then select the Share Select Playlists radio button control. Next, place check marks next to the playlists you want to share.

Now when someone is accessing your shared music over the network, they'll only be able to access the playlists that you've made available to them.

Secure Sharing

At the bottom of the Sharing controls in the iTunes Preferences windows are some additional entries. For example, you can enter a name for the music you're sharing in the Shared Name entry box. This can be anything you like, although it's probably a good idea to have it be meaningful enough that the folks around you will have some idea what it is when it pops up in their iTunes source list. (You can also give it a totally silly name, so it's a little more fun when *that* pops up in their source list.)

If you want to make sure your list of songs doesn't fall into the wrong hands, you can require a password in order to access the music. (If you have a wireless network, for instance, someone could conceivably sit out front in their car and access your shared library or playlists with an iBook or something else.) To activate password protection, place a check mark next to the Require Password entry box and then enter a password in that box. Now, you'll need to tell everyone what that password is.

Status

Finally, to implement any changes in the iTunes Preference window, you'll need to click OK. Note that you may see a dialog box that warns you that Sharing should be for personal use only. Click OK to dismiss the dialog box. If you'd prefer not to see this dialog box again (at some point in the future when you change the Sharing settings), click the Don't Show Again checkbox before clicking OK.

When you do, whatever choices about sharing you've made will be put into action. That means (as you'll see in the next section) that your iTunes Library or playlists may pop up in other people's iTunes source lists.

If you'd like to see if sharing has been activated and how things are going, just reopen iTunes Preferences and click the Sharing icon again. At the bottom of the window you'll see the Status entry, which tells you whether or not Sharing is turned on (On or Off) and how many users are connected. (A connected user is someone who has looked at your library or playlist or who is listening to one of your songs.)

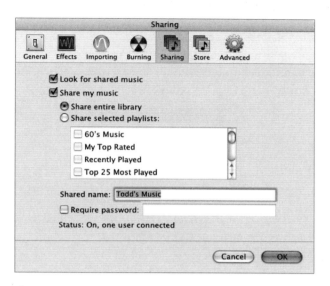

Play Shared Songs

In order to play shared songs, your copy of iTunes has to find the computer that's doing the sharing. That requires two things. First, you need to be attached to a TCP/IP-based network where a computer with a copy of iTunes is sharing music. Second, your computer needs to be properly configured to connect to that network. Third, you need to turn on the option in iTunes that causes it to look for shared music. To do that, open iTunes Preferences and click the Sharing icon. In the Sharing window, make sure the option Look For Shared Music has a check mark next to it and then click OK to close the Preferences window.

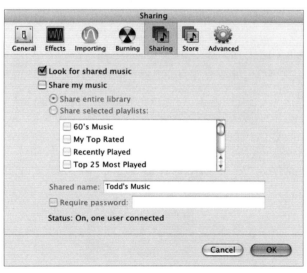

Access the Shared Music

Now, you can check and see if the shared music appears in your source list. If it does, then you're ready to start playing that shared music. Click the entry on your source list to access it.

> **NOTE**   *If the shared library or playlists are guarded by a password, then a dialog box will appear. Enter the password that was created for these shared songs and click OK.*

Next, if an entire library has been shared, then selecting it in the source list should reveal all the songs in that shared library (see Figure 7-4), just as it would if you selected your own Library icon in the source list. To play a song, select one in the main list and click the Play button or press the spacebar. All of the normal controls apply. The only thing you can't do with songs in a shared library is move them—even to a playlist and definitely not to your library or anywhere that would enable you to keep the songs on your computer.

> **TIP**   *Interestingly, you can browse a shared library the same way you browse your own library, by clicking the Browse button in the iTunes window or choosing Edit | Show Browser. You can't browse a shared playlist, however, just as you can't browse regular playlists.*

What if all you're sharing is playlists? In that case, what you'll see when you click the name of the shared music entry is nothing—except a disclosure triangle. Click that disclosure triangle next to the entry in the source list and you'll see the playlists revealed.

7

FIGURE 7-4   If you're sharing an entire library, you'll see it when you select the shared music entry.

Now you can select one of those playlists and play it back just as if it were one of your own—except you can't change them or move songs out of them. You can use the Control | Shuffle command, the various Continue commands, and so on to mix up the playback.

NOTE   *Shared Libraries and playlists are updated on the fly, so when the person with the "server" copy of iTunes makes changes to a library or playlist, it'll be reflected on the computers that are sharing that music. Likewise, changes in smart playlists will be reflected on the computers that are sharing them.*

While you're playing back songs that you're sharing, you may occasionally have a problem—network traffic or a slowdown affects your ability to get the MP3 stream, resulting in a problem. You may see a dialog box telling you that iTunes needs to "rebuffer" the song (in other words, it needs to wait to pre-load more of the song before it can continue playing it).

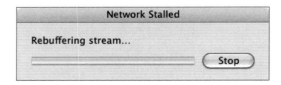

Disconnect

Want to disconnect from a shared music server? It's easily done. Select the entry in the source list and choose Controls | Disconnect, or press ⌘-E in Mac OS X (CTRL-E in Windows) or click the Eject button in the bottom-right corner of the iTunes window.

Of course, the server computer can also opt to stop sharing, in which case a song can end in the middle and the server's listing can disappear from the source list without warning. If the serving computer shuts down, restarts, or goes to sleep, the sharing will end abruptly as well. If you're turning off sharing, you'll see a warning dialog, but it doesn't give you an opportunity to warn those who are sharing your music that it's about to disappear.

iTunes Preference Settings

In this section, I'd like to take a look at all of the preference settings that iTunes makes available to us in the Preferences window—all of them. Some of these have been covered in greater detail in other sections and I'll refer you to those sections, but I think it'll be handy to have a quick look at all these different preference settings in one place.

Of course, to launch iTunes Preferences, choose iTunes | Preferences on the Mac or Edit | Preferences in the Windows version. When you do, you'll see the main Preferences window. This is one of the few interface elements that looks dramatically different between the Mac and Windows versions, although the options and settings themselves, for the most part, are identical. Figure 7-5 shows both operating systems.

At the top of the Preferences window are the icons that enable you to see the different groups of settings. If you've read earlier chapters, you've already encountered some of the settings on each of these. In this chapter, we've already looked at sharing extensively. To learn about the others, let's take a quick tour.

General Settings

Click the General icon (actually, the Preferences window opens to General by default) and you'll see some appearance and behavior options that might interest you. Here's a rundown:

7

- **Source Text and Song Text**   Use these menus to choose whether you want large or small text used for the Source Text (the text in the source list) or the Song Text (text in the main listing area) menus. The smaller the text,

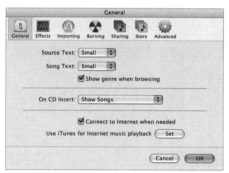

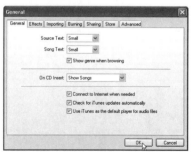

FIGURE 7-5   On the top is the Mac version of iTunes Preferences; on the bottom is what iTunes Preferences looks like in Windows.

the more songs or items you can see in a list; the larger the text, the easier it is to read. (So we've been told.)

- **Show genre when browsing**   With this option unchecked, you'll see only the Artist and Album columns when you click the Browse button (or choose Edit | Show Browser) in order to browse through your library. This can be handy because it gives you more room in those columns to see the full names of artists and albums (see Figure 7-6).

- **On CD Insert**   This menu enables you to choose from some interesting possibilities for automatic behavior that can result from inserting an audio CD. By default, the setting is to Show Songs, which simply mounts the CD in the iTunes interface and shows you the songs as discussed in Chapter 1. But you've got other choices, too. Select Begin Playing if you want the CD to automatically start playing at track one when it's inserted. Choose Import Songs if you want the mounted CD to automatically import songs, or choose Import Songs And Eject, which is a great little trick if you're trying to quickly import a number of CD's worth of songs to build your iTunes Library.

- **Connect to Internet When Needed**   Turn this option on if you want to allow iTunes to connect to the Internet to get CD track names from the Gracenotes CDDB database or to access the Music Store.

FIGURE 7-6   An example of browsing the library without the Genre column

- **Use iTunes for Internet music playback**   (Windows command is: *Use iTunes as default player for audio files.*) Click the Set button if you want to make it so that iTunes is used to play back streaming MP3s.

- **Check for iTunes updates automatically (Windows only)**   This option enables iTunes for Windows to check for updates from Apple when it has an active Internet connection.

Effects Settings

On the Effects preferences screen, you'll find just a few options, but they can have a fairly significant impact on what you hear when iTunes plays songs. Here's a look:

- **Crossfade playback**   Turn this option on by placing a check mark next to its box. Now, songs in your library or in playlists will fade between one another as a transition from one song to the next, almost as if a DJ were bringing down the level of one song and bringing up the level of another. You can use the slider control to determine how many seconds worth of the songs should overlap; the default is six seconds, but you can make the determination yourself.

- **Sound Enhancer**   Apple describes this feature as "adding depth and enlivening the quality of your music." Some users of iTunes report really liking the results, while others feel that it distorts the songs that they're hearing, particularly when connected to an external receiver or really good speakers. You can make up your own mind—click the checkbox next to Sound Enhancer to turn it on or off. Then, use the slider to change the level of sound enhancement.

> **TIP**   *You can actually turn the Sound Enhancer on and off and change the level while a song is playing to get an immediate sense of what's happening and what changes are occurring. In my opinion, it is helpful for small speakers and headphones, but it can be too much of a good thing when it comes to songs that were recorded with a great deal of reverb or that were performed in a concert-hall setting.*

- **Sound Check**   Turn on this option if you'd like iTunes to attempt to equalize the volume levels of songs as they're played. The idea here is to get songs that were recorded very loud and songs that were recorded very soft to play at a volume level that is closer to one another. While it works okay (particularly for background playback), you may find that a better long-term solution is to select individual songs that were recorded at odd levels and change their volume levels in the Info window. (Select a song and choose File | Get Info and click the Options tab.)

Importing Options

Some of these were discussed in detail in Chapter 1, but they're worth looking at more closely since there's actually a little digging you can do here to improve your importing experience:

- **Import Using** Choose the type of files you'd like to create when you import CD tracks in iTunes. The default in the latest versions of iTunes is the AAC Encoder, but you might want to import songs in different formats for different reasons. You can set this to MP3 Encoder, for instance, if you'd prefer to import songs as MP3s. (MP3s are more compatible with other applications and external devices, and they are, at this time, more common than AAC.) You might also want to use iTunes for other types of importing—say, AIFF or WAV files—and you can use this setting to change that.

> **NOTE** *The setting in the Import Using menu determines the exact nature of the Convert Selection command in the Advanced window of iTunes. If you choose to Import Using MP3 Encoder, for instance, the convert command will be Advanced | Convert Selection To MP3. This little trick even works for AIFF and WAV files.*

- **Setting** In the Setting menu, you can choose the quality setting for the encoder you've chosen. The options in the menu will include the defaults for that particular encoder, although you can also choose Custom from the menu and make selections to customize the level at which the songs will be encoded. (More on this in Chapter 9.)

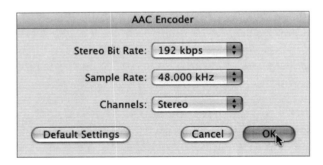

> **TIP** *The details window in the Importing preferences shows you what your current settings are in specifics that the Setting menu can't show you.*

- **Play songs while importing**   Select this option if you'd like to hear the songs on the audio CD as they're being imported; note that having this turned on can slow down the importing process somewhat.

- **Create file names with track number**   The behind-the-scenes files that iTunes creates when it encodes songs have to be named—generally, they'll be named after the song's title, but with this option active, the songs can also have the track number as part of the file name.

- **Use error correction when reading Audio CDs**   By default, this option is not turned on, but you can try it if you're having trouble with the audio quality of the songs that iTunes is creating. It slows down the process, but it may be a valid solution if you're hearing problems with the files that iTunes is creating.

Burning Settings

The options behind the Burning icon enable you to make decisions about how iTunes will interact with your CD or DVD burner. If your burner is built into your Mac, then iTunes should have relatively little trouble with it. Working with external and third-party burners can sometimes require a bit more tweaking, which you can accomplish with these settings. Of course, it's here that you'll also choose the type of CD you want to burn, as was discussed in Chapter 2.

- **CD-Burner**   Here you'll see the name of recognized CD (or DVD) burners. If you have more than one burner attached and recognized by this Mac, you can choose the default from this menu. (If you only have one, you won't see a menu.)

- **Preferred Speed**   Generally, your preferred speed is the Maximum Possible, but you might also select a different speed if you experience problems burning the CDs from iTunes. If you encounter failures, try a lower speed setting to see if that can help.

- **Disc Format**   This option is actually three radio buttons: Audio CD, MP3 CD, and Data CD, or DVD. You'll choose one of those options to determine the type of CD you're going to create in iTunes—see Chapter 2 for details.

TIP   *Notice that the Audio CD radio button, when selected, activates two other options—you can set a gap between songs and you can opt to have iTunes use Sound Check. When you turn on Use Sound Check, iTunes will attempt to equalize the volume levels of the songs that are being burned to the CD.*

Sharing Settings

In the sharing settings, you'll find the settings that enable you to share your library or selected playlists with others on your local network (whether Mac or PC). These settings are discussed extensively in the section "Rendezvous and iTunes Library Sharing" earlier in this chapter.

Store Settings

Store settings enable you to govern how iTunes will behave when you're accessing the iTunes Music Store. They include the following:

- **Show iTunes Music Store**   This one is turned on by default, but if you click to remove the check mark, the Music Store will disappear from your source list. When it's on, you have two other radio button choices—Buy and Download Using 1-Click and Buy Using a Shopping Cart. The 1-Click approach uses a credit card and billing information that's associated with your Apple ID to buy any songs you order; the Shopping Cart approach will put songs in a shopping cart and enable you to buy—and then download—the songs all at once.

- **Play Songs After Downloading**   Turn on this option if you want songs to begin playing automatically right after they've been purchased and downloaded.

- **Load Complete Preview Before Playing**   Sometimes if you attempt to listen to the preview of a song in the iTunes Music Store over a low-bandwidth Internet connection, you'll encounter streaming errors and rebuffering. The solution is to ask iTunes to download the entire sample before playing it. This can take a long time over a modem, but it may be the best solution if streaming is giving you trouble. (Indeed, the iTunes Music Store experience can be frustrating for some modem users regardless of the settings choices you make—it's an application that begs for a faster connection.)

Advanced Settings

The Advanced settings are terribly expansive, but they hide a few little tidbits. Some of these are covered elsewhere, but here's a quick round-up:

- **iTunes Music Folder Location**   Click the Change button to change the location where iTunes stores its music files; click Reset to set it to the default location. (See Chapter 8 for more discussion on storing and moving an iTunes library.)

- **Streaming Buffer Size**   Choose the size of the buffer for streaming MP3 feeds, including Internet radio stations. If you find that stations have to rebuffer or encounter other playback errors often, set this to Large. It will take longer for the station or MP3 stream to begin playback, but the playback itself may be smoother.

- **Shuffle By**   When you select the Shuffle command in the Controls menu, you can have it shuffle by song or by album. When you choose by song, you'll get a truly random mix of your library or playlist; when you choose by album, you'll change the order of the albums that are played back, but you'll hear each album in its entirety before moving to the next one.

- **Keep iTunes Music Folder organized**   With this option checked, iTunes attempts to organize your iTunes folder by artist and then by album, even for songs that are purchased or imported separate from an entire album. With this option turned off, songs are added to your iTunes Music folder in a more haphazard way.

- **Copy files to iTunes Music folder when added to library**   If you turn this option off, imported music won't necessarily be copied to your iTunes folder, although files imported from audio CDs still will be. This enables you to play songs that are on other parts of your hard disk (or other hard disks attached to your Mac) without duplicating the songs in your iTunes Music folder.

- **Show iTunes icon in the system tray (Windows only)**   Turn on this option if you'd like iTunes to place an icon on the Windows System Tray, which makes it convenient to launch and control iTunes when the window isn't available.

7

Chapter 8

iTunes Under the Hood

How to...

- Understand the File Hierarchy
- Switch, Move, and Restore a Library
- Manage Your Growing Library

iTunes goes to some effort to make sure the behind-the-scenes stuff that it does (converting files, moving them around, organizing them into folders and hierarchies) is relatively invisible to the casual user. And it is, for the most part. But if you'd like to go beyond being a "casual user" of iTunes—and if you'd like to dig in and access the files that iTunes is creating and managing—it'll require a look at what's going on behind the scenes in iTunes' hierarchy of folders. We explore that file hierarchy in this chapter. When you start accumulating a seriously large library of files, you may run into other thorny issues as well, some of which we'll cover here.

Finally, iTunes not only manages the digital audio files you already have, but it creates new files—particularly when you import songs and audio files from CDs or other media—and copies files from one place to another. We'll examine those settings in a little more depth than we have so far.

Understand the iTunes File Hierarchy

We've explored iTunes as a digital music player, as a digital music converter, and even as an online store application. At its heart, however, this "jukebox" application is really a digital music *management* utility. One thing that is going on in the background whenever you add music to your library (or when you choose to translate or copy or buy a new song or album from the iTunes Music Store) is that music is being organized into the iTunes database and, in many cases, copied and moved about in the underlying hierarchy of files and folders that iTunes creates.

As users, we can control some of iTunes' management techniques. We can set the default location for the iTunes Library, for instance, and we can tell iTunes whether or not we want all of the files that it manages to be copied to that location. We can also determine, at least a little bit, how iTunes organizes its underlying folders. To get a handle on those items, however, we should back up and take a look at how iTunes stores files.

The iTunes Hierarchy

By default, iTunes stores its library in your personal Music files, whether you're working in Windows or Mac OS X. For Mac users, that folder is called Music, and it's located in your home folder (/users/*yourname*/Music/), as shown in Figure 8-1.

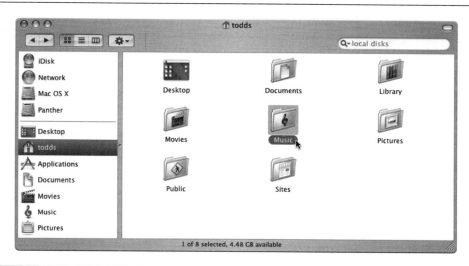

FIGURE 8-1   The Music file in Mac OS X

8

For Windows users, the folder where your iTunes files are saved is called My Music, and it's located in your personal documents folder (C:\Documents and Settings\Owner\My Documents\My Music). The easiest way to access it is by choosing My Music from the Start menu. It's shown in Figure 8-2.

NOTE   *Your My Music folder may be located in a slightly different place if you've configured more than one user on your Windows computer. If this is the case, it might be found in C:\Documents and Settings\Username\My Documents\.*

If you've installed iTunes, then you'll likely see a folder inside the Music or My Music folder called, simply, iTunes. That's where iTunes will put all if its files, both its internal database and any digital audio files that it imports or copies for use in the library. You can see, when you dig into the iTunes folder, that it contains both support files and the iTunes Music folder, which is where the digital audio files are managed and stored. (This illustration shows the Mac OS X Columns View, which is handy for seeing how it looks to drill down into the iTunes folder.)

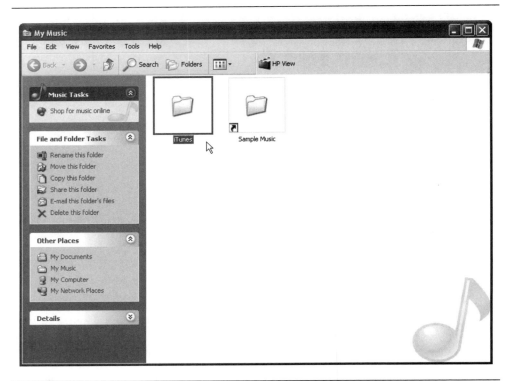

FIGURE 8-2   The My Music folder in Windows XP

The file, iTunes 4 Music Library, is the database file that iTunes uses to manage the library and playlists, while the file, `iTunes Music Library.xml`, is an Extensible Markup Language file that contains tons of information about your iTunes library, which can be useful for developers and third-party applications. (XML is a standard format for data exchange, so it's easy for someone knowledgeable to write a utility program that can work with the names of songs, artists, albums and other data about your iTunes Library and playlists.) The iTunes Music folder is where iTunes stores the digital audio files that you purchase from the iTunes Music Store and that you import from CDs. Songs are also stored here if you've turned on the Copy Files To iTunes Music Folder option in the Advanced settings of iTunes Preferences.

In the iTunes Music folder, by default, you'll find a listing of the artists that have songs (or other audio files) stored in your iTunes database. When you select one of those artists, you'll see the albums that you have stored for that artist. This list doesn't include just the complete albums you've imported—any album from which you have one song will be listed here.

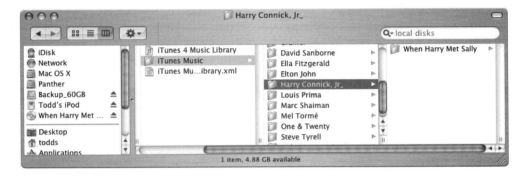

Finally, if you select an album, you'll see a listing of all the songs on that album. In fact, in the Mac OS, you can select a song and, if you're in Columns view in the Finder, you can play that song from within the Finder window.

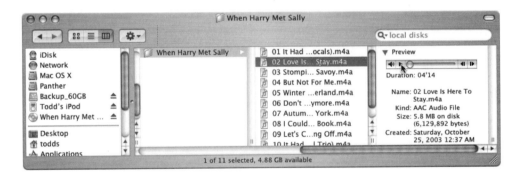

In Mac OS X or Windows, you can even double-click the song to launch it in iTunes and play it back. (It may launch in a different application if iTunes isn't your default playback application for MP3 or AAC digital audio files.)

Library Management Options

When I was first explaining the iTunes hierarchy of folders, I started it by saying that it works this way "by default." The truth is, the Artist | Album | Songs approach isn't necessarily the only way that iTunes is willing to manage songs that you import. You can also set it so that it's a bit less organized in its approach. In the iTunes Preferences, choose Advanced and turn off the Keep iTunes Music Folder

 **Determine a Song's Location**

As you can tell from this discussion, it's not always an easy matter to find a particular song on your hard disk. Not only is it buried in the folders that iTunes created for managing these files, but it may also be located in a different place altogether, such as a shared folder on your multiuser system or in a special location on your network.

Fortunately, iTunes makes it easy to find out where a song's file is actually stored. If you're goal is to learn the path to the file, select a song and choose File | Get Info from iTunes' menu. In the Info window, on the Summary tag, you can see the path to this file's location at the bottom of the window in the area labeled Where.

If you're just interested in having the file pop up in the Finder or in Windows Explorer, then select the song in the library (or in a playlist, but not on an iPod or CD) and choose File | Show Song File. (You can also select the song and press either ⌘-R on a Mac or CTRL-R in Windows, or you can right-click in Windows or CONTROL-click on a Mac and select Show Song File from the contextual menu.) The folder holding that song should appear on your screen, and the song file will be front and center (on a Mac, it's highlighted; in Windows, you'll simply see the contents of the folder that holds the file).

Organized option which will keep iTunes from moving files around in the iTunes Music folder and organizing them by artist and album.

The other thing that's important to know is that your songs don't have to be stored in this hierarchy—all of the songs that you import from CDs or buy from the iTunes Music Store will be, but other songs that were already on your hard disk don't have to be copied to your iTunes folder and they don't have to be organized by iTunes in the way that imported songs are—although they can be. If you have songs that you'd like to add to your library, but they're located elsewhere on your hard disk or even on an external hard disk, you can still add them to your library without copying them in the iTunes folder hierarchy. Open iTunes Preferences and click the Advanced icon. In the Advanced options, make sure that the option Copy Files To iTunes Music Folder When Adding To Library is turned off.

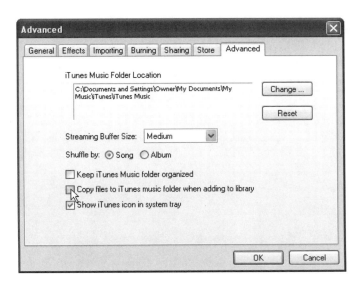

Now when you add songs to your library that are elsewhere on a local or external disk, those files will stay on that disk and you can still play them back.

The other option among the Advanced settings that we're interested in here is the Keep iTunes Music Folder Organized option. If it's turned off, you can organize songs that you store in the folder yourself without interference from iTunes—in other words, if you'd prefer to go into the iTunes Music folder and create folders for Rock, R&B, and Jazz and then store folders full of songs or albums or artists that way, iTunes can actually deal with that just fine. As long you don't delete music files, iTunes can find them even if you move them around on the hard disk. In this example, I've turned off the option and opted to organize my songs the way I want them (by style or genre) in the iTunes Music folder:

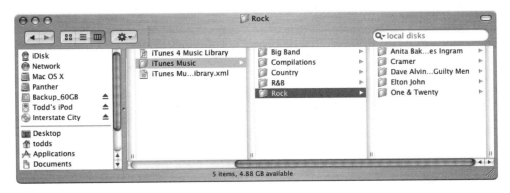

8

The songs will continue to be organized that way as long as I don't turn on the Keep iTunes Music Folder Organized option. If you do turn on the option after making your own changes and creating folder hierarchies in the folder, you'll see a dialog box like this one:

Click Yes if you'd like iTunes to begin organizing all of your songs according to its system again. (iTunes will even delete any folders that don't fit into its scheme after it has moved your songs out of them to other folders!) Click No if you don't mind it using its system for new songs but you want to keep your own system for your old stuff.

Change the Music Folder Location

Another quick feature in iTunes Preference's Advanced settings is the option to change the location of your iTunes Music folder. If you don't like having it in your Music or My Music folder, you can change it. iTunes will use the new location that you specify for new music files it creates when importing from an audio CD or after a purchase from the iTunes Music Store.

Why do this? It can be handy if your regular computer or laptop has a small hard disk and you'd like to use an external drive for storing your music collection. Or, perhaps you want to store song files in a shared folder where others can access them. In both Mac OS X and Windows XP, this can be a good idea if you have your computer set up for multiple users. Note, however, that the default choice—having a local iTunes Music folder on your startup disk—is the easiest to manage for synchronizing and so on. If you change the default, you may occasionally need to move files around to keep iTunes up-to-date.

To make the change, open iTunes Preferences and choose the Advanced button. Now, click the Change button next to the iTunes Music Folder Location box. You'll see an Open dialog box that you can use to locate the folder you want to use for the music. For instance, in this example, I'm choosing a folder that's in the Shared folder on a Mac OS X installation—this is a folder that anyone can access, even when they're logged into a different account on this computer. That makes the music files available to anyone who is logged into this Mac.

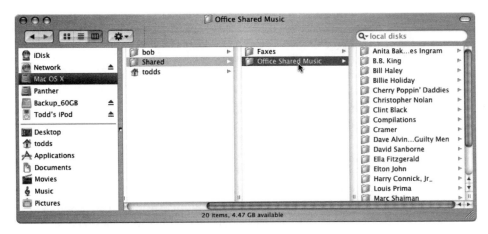

This dialog box is a little different in Windows since it uses a standard Windows dialog box instead of one written by Apple. Use the window to locate the folder you'd like to use for your music files. Note that you can click the Make New Folder button if you want to create a folder somewhere for the digital audio files.

Once you make the change, iTunes will ask you to confirm that this is what you want to do. Note that, by default, none of your existing files are actually moved to the new location—iTunes just needs to update its database.

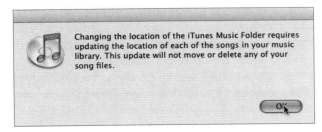

Now, any new music that you import or buy will be added to the new location, although your existing files stay where they are in the original iTunes Music folder. You can, however, copy those files to the new location if you'd like. What I would recommend is that you open up the iTunes Music folder and then drag all of the folders that are named after artists into the new shared music folder. iTunes can pick up and organize those folders for you if you have the Keep iTunes Music Folder Organized option turned on.

Move, Restore, and Consolidate a Library

One great thing about how iTunes manages songs is the fact that it's flexible in terms of how you get the songs into iTunes. Simply dragging a folder full of songs to the iTunes Library window works fine—iTunes will take a look at what it is that you're dragging and will add the songs to the library, even if they're in folders. Neither the folders nor the hierarchy or organization of the songs matter, because iTunes will simply arrange them in the library by artist, album, and song name—which you can then search, browse, and add to playlists any way you want.

So, this flexibility is the answer to a few questions, such as how do you move a library of songs from one computer to another? And how can you restore from a backup if you run into trouble. Both can be done easily, with some caveats for protected songs, which you have to manage a bit more carefully. iTunes also includes a special command, the Consolidate Library command, which you can use to put all of your songs in one place.

Move Your Library

If you're literally *moving* the songs, say from your old computer to a new one, then the first order of business is to put your library on something that you can move—an external hard disk, a data CD, or even a data DVD. Just make sure that your target computer can handle whatever media you decide on. You'll then want to copy the files to that media—if you happen to know that all of the songs have been stored in your iTunes Music folder, then backing it up is easy. If they haven't been stored there, then creating a data CD or DVD might be a good idea so you'll have all your song files collected in one place.

> NOTE　*Creating occasional data CDs or DVDs of your entire music library is a good idea in case your hard disk runs into trouble and you can't recover your songs. Creating a data CD or DVD is discussed in Chapter 3.*

If a disc is an impractical solution—say, you've got a large library and don't have a DVD burner—then you can try something else. First, you can set your iTunes

Music Folder to another location—for instance, an external hard disk—using the Advanced settings in the iTunes Preferences. Change the location for the iTunes Music Folder as described earlier in this chapter.

Once the new music folder has been set, choose the command Advanced | Consolidate Library. What this command does is copy all of the songs that are in your library to your music folder. (Remember, iTunes doesn't copy all files to the library by default, so the songs may be in many different locations.) Because you just changed your library's location to the external hard disk, all of your songs will be copied there.

NOTE   *In fact, you could now switch your music folder back to its original location in the Advanced settings of iTunes and all of the songs you copied to that external disk would still be there as a backup or as a mirror image that you could use with other computers.*

Now, one important step should be taken if (1) you're planning to move this library to a new computer for good and (2) you've ever bought music from the iTunes Music Store. You should choose the command Advanced | Deauthorize Computer in the iTunes menu. You'll see a dialog box asking you if you want to deauthorize the computer for an Apple account or an Audible.com account. Make your choice (probably Apple account if we're talking about items that you've purchased via the iTunes Music Store) and click OK. A deauthorized computer can't play songs that you bought using your Apple ID. But, more importantly, deauthorizing one computer makes it possible for you to use another computer to play back those songs—only three computers can be authorized at a time. Because of this, you'll probably want to free up the computer you're leaving behind so you can listen to purchased songs on your new machine.

Now, with your songs on an external disk, here's what you do:

1. Disconnect from the original computer and connect that drive to the computer that's the target for this library move.

2. With the disk (or other media) mounted on the target computer, launch iTunes on the target computer and open iTunes Preferences.

3. Select Advanced and then turn on the option Copy Files To iTunes Music Folder When Adding To Library. You should also verify that the iTunes Music Folder Location is set to the place where you want these files to end up after they're copied from the external disk. Click OK.

4. Now, in iTunes, make sure the library is selected in the source list.

5. In the Finder or Windows Explorer, open up the external disk and locate the iTunes Music folder that you created on the external disk. Now, drag all of the songs from the disk to the library main list in iTunes. Note, as shown in Figure 8-3, that you can simply drag the Library folder or iTunes Music or whatever you called the main folder and drop it on the library list. iTunes will automatically find all of the music files in that folder and add them to the library.

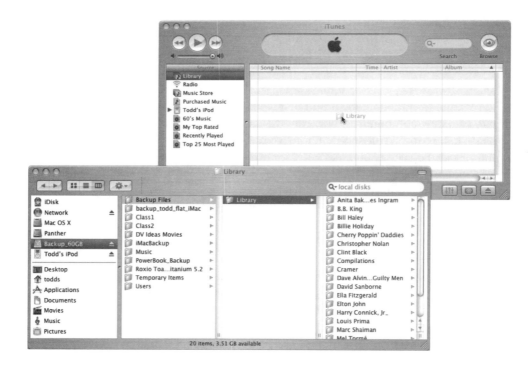

FIGURE 8-3   To add your complete library to iTunes on a different computer, drag and drop your entire archived, consolidated music folder to iTunes.

NOTE

Occasionally, in all of this moving around, you'll encounter a circumstance where you lose the metadata—which means data about data—regarding a song. As a result, once iTunes imports songs from one disk to another, you end up without titles, artist information, and other details regarding that particular song. There are, however, some steps you can take to fix this. See Chapter 11 for details.

Restore Your Library

Restoring a library is pretty much the same as moving one, except that you'll likely be dealing with a backup of your library, or you may be attempting to restore it from different locations, such as an external drive and some data CDs that you've made. To restore the library, simply drag items from the various locations into the library's main list (see Figure 8-4). If you want to have all of those items copied to your iTunes Music folder, choose Advanced | Consolidate Library and any files that weren't already copied to your iTunes Music folder will then be copied.

8

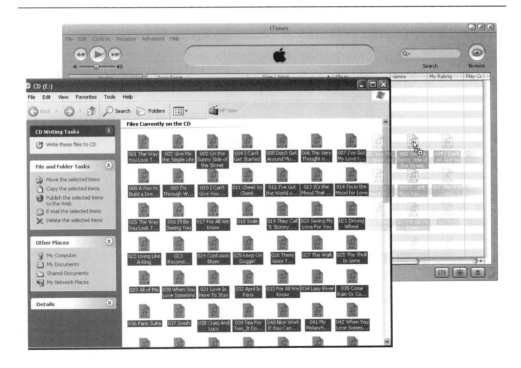

FIGURE 8-4   Restoring from a backup data CD to the iTunes Library in Windows

 *The library that you restore to does not have to be completely empty. You can always drag songs from a removable disc or an external hard disk into a library that has some songs in it and not create any problems. You may still want to run the Consolidate Library command, however, if your interest is in getting all those songs to the same place on your hard disk.*

Manage Your Growing Library

Although MP3s and AAC files are certainly an efficient way to store music and spoken recordings, it still doesn't take all that long to fill up a few gigabytes of storage space and, depending on your Mac model, your interest in music, and the other files you have hanging around, you may soon find you're running out of storage space.

Storage space tends to be the biggest problem when it comes to managing a large library of songs. iTunes had more trouble in earlier versions, but now it no longer has any practical limit to the number of songs that can be placed in an iTunes Library, so there's no cause for concern even if you find you have thousands of songs stored on your hard disk. Unless, of course, you're starting to exceed the capacity of that disk.

Any solution to this problem is a workaround. Here are a few thoughts:

- **Put files on an external drive**   As we discussed earlier in the chapter, iTunes can work just fine with its iTunes Music folder located elsewhere on a network, on an external drive, or something similar. So, to increase your Mac's ability to deal with more music, simply transfer your iTunes Music folder to a larger external hard disk and then play the songs from that disk. The only problem you'll have is when the disk isn't available to your Mac, and iTunes reacts fairly well under those circumstances, giving you a dialog box that tells you the song can't be located. The song isn't deleted from the iTunes Library, and you won't encounter much extra trouble. In fact, songs that can't be found simply appear in the library with a small exclamation point until they're located or the original location is mounted again.

	☑ I Feel Fine	2:18	The Beatles	1
❶	☑ Eight Days A Week	2:44	The Beatles	1
	☑ Ticket To Ride	3:10	The Beatles	1
	☑ Help!	2:18	The Beatles	1
	☑ Yesterday	2:05	The Beatles	1

- **Split your library**   This one is a little tougher to manage, but say you have a small hard disk in your laptop, for instance, and a larger external hard disk that you don't always want to take with you. If you set your default iTunes Music folder to the external drive, you can use it for more of the files that you add to iTunes. You can then manually add your favorites to a folder on your laptop. (Put them in a special playlist, too, that is comprised only of the locally saved songs.) As far as iTunes is concerned, when the external disk is connected, a song on the external disk is no different than one on the internal disk. When you hit the road, though, you can just play songs that you've organized in the special locally saved playlist.

■ **Use a data CD or data DVD**   A data CD can hold hours and hours of music; a DVD can hold weeks' worth. If you have a portion of your library that you're pretty happy with and that doesn't need to be altered much, you can burn it to CD or DVD and then play songs from that disc via iTunes. This works pretty well for desktops that happen not to have a lot of storage space. Plus, it encourages you to back up your music library to disc. If there's a drawback, it's that discs aren't the best solution for portables on battery power. It takes less power to play songs off your hard disk than it does from a CD or DVD.

■ **Use an iPod**   An iPod is a great way to extend your library beyond the limits of your internal hard disk. The latest iPods offer a huge capacity that you can work with, after all. The key is to use your iPod in manual mode, as discussed in Chapter 6. Not only does that allow you to freely manage songs between your library and iPod, but you can play songs directly from your iPod as well (see Figure 8-5). If you do take this approach, remember that your imported files are still going to be saved to the library, so you'll want to delete them (and have them moved to the trash upon deletion) if you're storing items on your iPod in order to keep your hard disk cleared.

CAUTION   *If you use your iPod as your main library, it's very important to back up songs that you've stored on your iPod. After all, the iPod is a device that can conceivably be lost, dropped, or run over with a car—so you should have backups of your imported and purchased songs on data CDs or similar, just in case you lose your iPod.*

■ **Make your songs smaller**   If storage space is more important than crystal clear quality, you can dig into your iTunes settings and opt to have your songs saved at a lower quality level. Open iTunes Preferences and click the Importing button. Now, choose a new setting in the Setting menu—a lower kbps level will help for starters. (For instance, while 128 kbps is considered "good" MP3 quality, you can probably get away with 96 kbps and it will still sound like something approaching FM radio quality. Plus, with 96 kbps, you get about a 25 percent savings in storage space for the music file.)

8

FIGURE 8-5   With an iPod in manual mode, you can play songs, move them around, and manage playlists (or play songs from them, as shown).

Beyond the kbps level, you can also decrease the sample rate—while 44.1 KHz is CD-quality, 24 KHz can be OK if you're trying to get your songs smaller. To change sample rates and dig further into the encoding options, choose Custom from the Setting menu. You'll see a dialog box like the one shown in Figure 8-6.

NOTE   *If you change these settings to make some of the songs smaller in your current library, you can then select the songs and choose the Advanced | Convert Select command to convert a song to the new settings. Remember, however, to change these settings back if you prefer to use the higher quality settings for importing from CDs. It's a good idea to get a high-quality song file, burn it to a data CD for backup, then convert it to something smaller for storing on your hard disk if you're pressed for space. That way, you'll still have the high-quality version stored for access later.*

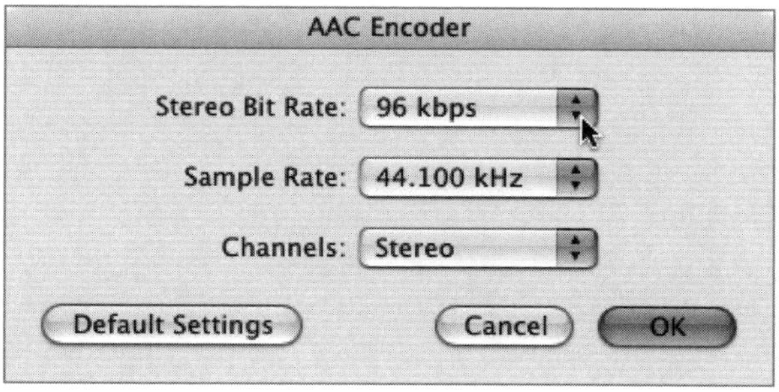

FIGURE 8-6 Options for encoding an AAC file

Those are some thoughts for squeezing a large library onto a small (or shrinking) hard disk. For more in-depth discussions on encoding, translating, and working with AAC, MP3, and other digital audio files, turn to Chapter 9.

8

Chapter 9

Fun with Digital Audio Files

How to...

- Buy (or Subscribe) to Other Online Services
- Listen to Audio Books
- Dig Deeper into iTunes Encoding
- Create and Translate MP3s
- Edit Digital Audio Files
- Translate Analog Recordings to Digital

iTunes may be in a class by itself, but it's certainly not the first or only software to do a lot of what it's capable of. You'll find that Internet and computer stores have plenty of options when it comes to playing back digital audio, buying digital audio files (or listening to subscribed music), and creating MP3s. There are even specialty applications aimed at such tasks as turning songs on a vinyl record album into acceptable MP3 (and other digital audio format) files.

In this chapter, I'd like to pull together some slightly disparate ideas under the umbrella heading of "fun with digital audio files." We'll start by looking at some of the other services available for digital music downloading (the legal ones) as well as a glance at Audible.com, which makes books-on-tape available both through the iTunes Music Store and via its own service. Then, we'll head back into iTunes to take another look at the encoding options that enable you to import and translate audio files. From there, we'll take a look at some third-party applications and solutions that enable you to do a variety of things to your digital audio files such as translate them, edit them, or even create such files from scratch.

Buy (or Subscribe) to Other Online Services

One aspect of the iTunes experience that people either seem to love or hate is the iTunes Music Store. Most people (myself included) find it rather addicting, although it's certainly true that you can slam up against its limits, as the Store is far from having every recording every made. The iTunes Music Store was fairly unique when it launched, as few other services were offering the $0.99 (U.S.) per song approach that enables you to download and work with the audio file as you please. (Of course, Apple's iPod helped determine how that would work in one sense since Apple wanted to make sure your $0.99 enables you to move your song to the iPod and take it with you.) Until the iTunes Music Store, most people's MP3 experiences were limited to either subscription services that enable you to listen to songs and albums online or some form of file swapping that, to put it delicately, might infringe on copyright laws.

So the iTunes Music Store launched as a highly publicized competitor for both streaming MP3 services and illegal file swapping. At $0.99 per song, you could get benefits similar to file swapping, yet it was on the up-and-up. Plus, the advantage over streaming MP3 is that you could take the songs with you to another computer, on a burned audio CD or on your portable digital audio player. But, of course, the iTunes Music Store isn't the only choice and, due to the competitive, startup nature of digital music stores, you'll find that some stores have access to different music than does the iTunes Music Store. (Maybe one day one of the stores will have it all, but right now they have different agreements with various labels and publishers. If you want the best options, you may need to explore multiple services.)

NOTE *If you opt to use a different music service application for most of your playback, you can export your playlists from iTunes in a plain text format that, hopefully, other applications can read and use to replicate your playlists in the new application. Select File | Export Song List and choose where to save it using the Save dialog box that appears.*

9

MP3.com and EMusic

Today, you'll find that services offer all sorts of solutions along these lines, and some of them work well with iTunes. You can subscribe to streaming MP3 services, such as MP3.com, which enables you to listen to album tracks and entire albums using streaming MP3 technology. Once you're signed up, you can click a link to a stream and it will appear in your library in iTunes. Or, as shown in Figure 9-1, just clicking one of the Play Tracks Now buttons that you'll find on MP3.com will add tons of tracks to your iTunes Library, which you can then play back and manage at your leisure. You can even create a playlist and drag the stream link to that playlist, where you can access it again later. You can then listen to the streams again and again, as long as you've got an active Internet connection.

NOTE *You'll find that one thing that's happening as you're adding streams to iTunes is that they're being downloaded, initially to your web browser's default download folder—on a Mac, that's often the desktop, which can make a mess after a while. If you plan to access quite a few of these streams, you might want to dig into your browser's preference settings and change the default download folder.*

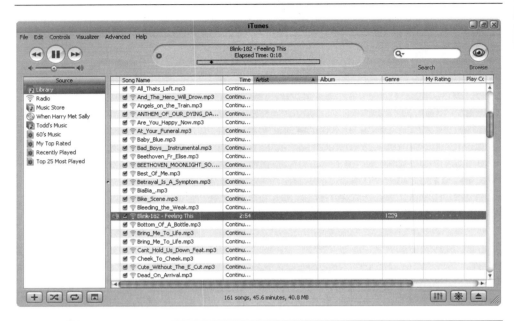

FIGURE 9-1   MP3.com dumping a bunch of MP3 streaming links into the iTunes Library

MP3.com has other features, too, such as some downloadable MP3s and "stations" that are customized playlists offered by MP3.com enthusiasts. It's a great service for staying on top of the very latest since much of it is driven by Top 40 charts and music news, as well as a strong focus on independent music and undiscovered artists, with special pages devoted to artists and their songs. Most of the service is free, although you can buy albums through MP3.com (you get the actual CD shipped to you as well as access to the music online), and MP3.com offers an ad-free option for (currently) $1.99 per month.

NOTE   *Many Windows-oriented iPods came with MusicMatch Jukebox, and it ships with a number of PCs as well. MusicMatch can be used for local playback, it can synchronize with an iPod, and it can be used to connect to the MusicMatch digital music service. It also has a music service that is subscription oriented. To enable the best features, you'll pay a monthly fee.*

MP3.com's sister service is eMusic.com, which is a straightforward subscription-based MP3 download service that gives you access to songs from independent record labels. In some ways, it's similar to the iTunes Music Store, except that you subscribe to the service, which enables you to download a certain number of songs (currently 40 downloads per month at $9.99 and 65 at $14.99). It's a better price than $0.99 per song, but only if you find enough songs to download. iTunes Music Store has deals with many major labels that eMusic.com does not. If you opt to use the service, you'll interact with it using the EMusic Download Manager. Actually, you pick the songs by selecting them in your web browser, and then choosing the Download control—when you do, control is handed to the EMusic Download Manager.

NOTE *In my experience with the EMusic Download Manager in Mac OS X, I had to manually enter a MIME type in the web browser. (Internet Explorer supports this; Safari doesn't.) You can set the MIME type in IE by opening its preferences and choosing File Helpers, then creating a new File Helper. Enter **application/vnd.emusic-emusic_package** for the MIME type, then **.emp** for the extension, and tell IE to handle the file by Post-Process With Application, then choose EMusic Download Manager as that application. In Safari, it appears that you'll need to double-click the downloaded EMusic file to get it to launch in EMusic Download Manager and, hence, download the song.*

BuyMusic.com

Windows users can visit Buymusic.com, which acts as a direct competitor to iTunes Music Store, offering songs for around $1 and albums for $9.99 and up. The store is highly reliant on Windows Media Player for playback and song management, and uses a shopping cart system (as opposed to a "one-click" system). Thus, selecting the songs places them in your shopping cart until you're ready to "check out," at which time it downloads all of your selections. (See Figure 9-2.)

NOTE *See Chapter 10 for more discussion regarding Windows Media Player.*

Napster 2.0

Want another name-brand option? How about Napster? The original Napster was one of the leaders in unpaid file sharing that lead to a whole bunch of MP3 swapping (as well as the extraordinary popularity of MP3 and digital audio files). After slogging through legal battles and selling the name, Napster 2.0 (www.napster.com), which is now owned by Roxio (makers of Toast and CD/DVD Creator products) is back with

FIGURE 9-2 BuyMusic.com lets you buy songs and play them back using Windows Media Player.

an iTunes Music Store–style proposition—songs for $0.99 per track and $9.95 per album (at this writing). Figure 9-3 shows Napster in action. Note that Napster 2.0 is a Windows 2000/XP–only service at this time.

With Napster 2.0, as with many music services, you begin by downloading the special Napster browser (shown in Figure 9-3). Once downloaded and installed, you can use the browser to look for music that interests you by choosing Browse mode or searching using the entry boxes in the top-right corner and clicking the Search button.

Napster 2.0 works a *lot* like iTunes. When you find a track that you want to sample, double-click it in the window and you'll hear a small 30-second sample. (You can control the playback of that sample in the top-right corner of the window.) You can actually use the interface to add song *samples* to your playlists, perhaps to remind you of songs that you want to purchase. When you click a Buy Now link (you can also right-click a song and choose Buy Song from the contextual menu), you'll see a dialog box that asks you for personal and credit card information to complete the sale.

FIGURE 9-3   Napster is another attempt at an iTunes Music Store killer.

Napster 2.0 also offers a premium subscription service that enables you to listen to streaming music using the interface. The service, which costs $9.95 per month (at this writing), is how you enable the Web radio features of Napster 2.0. And it works with a portable digital music device, but not the iPod. Instead, it's designed to work with a special Dell player that's specifically branded for the Napster 2.0 service.

Listen to Audio Books

The king of the MP3 audio book is Audible.com, with which Apple has partnered to make audio books available in the iTunes Music Store. On the iTunes Store, you buy audio books piecemeal, which you can do on the Audible.com site as well. But if you're a serious audio book junkie, you may also want to consider the Audible.com subscription service, which you pay for in monthly installments and that allows you to access either one or two audio books per month, plus other audio magazines, newspapers, and/or radio content. The subscription approach can save you some money as long as you take advantage of it monthly (great for commuters, I would think).

Buy a Book

If you purchase or retrieve Audible.com content directly from their web site, it's sent to iTunes in the same basic way that the iTunes Music Store sends audio files, so you should have no trouble locating a downloaded audio book in your library. In the Audible store, after you've gotten through the checkout process, you're given the opportunity to choose a file size and quality, and then download it. Once you've done so, it appears on your desktop or in your download folder. Double-click it and you'll switch to iTunes, which may ask you to enter your Audible.com account information. If you do that successfully, you'll see the audio book appear in your iTunes Library.

Song Name	Time	Artist ▲	Album	Genre	My Rating
☑ Lies (Unabridged), Part 1	4:16:34	Al Franken		Spoken Word	
☑ B.B. Boogie	3:17	B.B. King	How Blue Can You Get	Blues	

Audible.com files have a .aa filename extension, but playback is pretty much the same as playing back an MP3 or AAC file—simply double-click it to begin listening. You can drag an audio book to a playlist, if you like, and audio books are included in smart playlists as well. You might even select the Audible.com file and choose File | Get Info. There on the Summary screen (see Figure 9-4) you can see information about the book, including the bit rate, sample rate, and other info.

Finally, you can drag your audio book to your iPod if you'd like, although there is a caveat—audio books work a little differently than regular songs. The rule is that you can have audio books from no more than two accounts on your iPod at once. If you try to drag a book from a third account, it won't work. (I think that's probably to keep you from using a different name and signing up multiple times to take advantage of the cheap first-month deals you can get, although I may be mistaken.)

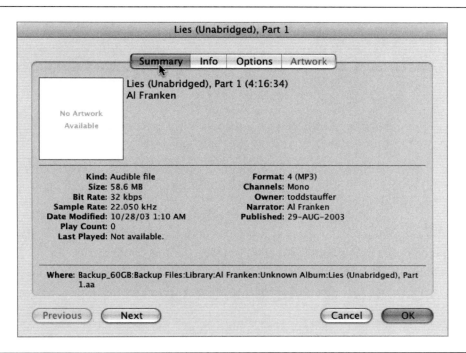

FIGURE 9-4   The Summary information for an audio book file

Burn a Book

You can burn an audio book to audio CD if you find that convenient for playback. What's more, the audio book can automatically be split across multiple CDs if it's too large to fit on a single CD. Here are the steps:

1. Open iTunes Preferences, click the Burning icon, and ensure that Audio CD is selected as the target type of CD to be burned. Click OK when you're done in iTunes Preferences.

2. To burn an audio book to CD, create a playlist and drag the audio book to that playlist. (Long audio books tend to be multiple files, so you can include all of them on the playlist if desired.)

3. Select the playlist and click the Burn icon. You'll be prompted for a blank disc. Enter one in your burner, and wait for iTunes to respond. If the audio book is longer than the CD's capacity, you'll see a dialog box telling you that multiple CDs can be created. Click the Audio CDs button to make that happen, or click Cancel if you'd prefer not to burn the audio book after all.

4. When the info window says it's ready, click the Burn icon again. iTunes will test the media, prepare the file, and begin writing to the audio disc.

5. When the first disc is completed, you'll be prompted to insert another (if appropriate). Follow the onscreen instructions to keep the burning process moving along.

When you're done, you'll have an audio CD—or a collection of audio CDs—that include your audio book. Now you're ready for that road trip.

Dig Deeper into iTunes Encoding

iTunes is actually impressively—if not surprisingly—powerful in its ability to translate between different types of digital audio files. The reason I say impressively is that iTunes is, at first glance, really a "jukebox" application—a program designed to manage and arrange digital audio files for playback in different and interesting ways. So it's surprising that iTunes is also able to encode and translate between quite a few different audio formats—or, at least, it would be if iTunes wasn't built on top of Apple's QuickTime technology, which is actually pretty adept at that sort of translation.

So, we end up with iTunes' ability to import digital audio files from CD-ROM in a variety of formats, such as AIFF, WAV, MP3, and AAC. As you've seen, which format you end up using for encoded songs is set in the iTunes Preferences window by selecting the Importing icon. That, in turn, affects the command Advanced | Convert Selection. Based on the setting in the iTunes Preferences, you can convert songs to and from all four file formats (as long as the songs—or audiobooks—aren't protected files), and you can get fairly sophisticated in your settings choices, as I'll detail in this section.

Why choose a different format? As you'll see as we work our way through them, each file format has its strengths. AAC is great with iTunes and the iPod, MP3 is commonly used for Internet audio, and AIFF and WAV are native formats that work well in Mac and Windows applications, respectively.

Also, it's worth noting that you'll always get better quality when you encode a song directly into a format as opposed to translating a file to that format. For instance, if you set iTunes to encode directly into MP3 format when it imports songs from CDs, you'll get better results than if you first encode the song as an AAC and later translate it into an MP3. The quality difference may not be overwhelming, but for certain listeners it will be noticeable.

Encode in AAC

In iTunes 4 and later, the default option for digital music files is AAC, also known as MPEG-4 AAC audio. (AAC is actually the codec—the compressor/ decompressor—that's being used on a file that's saved in the MPEG-4 audio file format. AAC can also be used to compress 3GGP audio as well, which is the international standard for multimedia over wireless phone networks and similar setups.) AAC, as an iTunes format, has the advantage of being highly compressible and still offering very high-quality reproduction—better than MP3 at the same bit rate. All of that means you get a better sounding song in a smaller file. If there's a drawback to AAC, it's that it's not MP3—and MP3 is more popular. Apple made a calculated decision to go with AAC in conjunction with the iTunes Music Store, however, which may have been because of both the quality and the security of the AAC format, which Apple can control a bit more tightly. (There may also have been some institutional pride involved, as Apple's QuickTime technology is part of the foundation of the MPEG-4 standard.)

To encode songs in AAC format, you don't have to do anything special if you haven't already made changes to iTunes' settings. By default, iTunes is designed to encode songs in AAC format at high quality. You can tweak those settings, however, by opening iTunes Preferences and clicking the Importing button. Make sure the Import Using menu says AAC Encoder and then choose open the Settings menu. By default, there's only one entry—High Quality (128 kbps). If you'd like to customize that, choose Custom from the menu. When you do, the AAC Encoder dialog box appears.

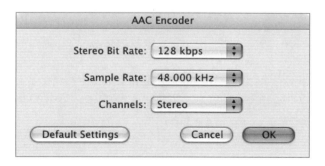

9

In this dialog box, you can make some choices (actually, relatively few, compared to other formats) about how your AAC file will be encoded. Here's a quick look:

■ The Stereo Bit Rate menu is where you'll get the most flexibility. You can choose a bit rate lower than the default 128 kbps if you'd like your songs to take up less disk space when stored, or choose a higher bit rate if space isn't an issue and you'd like a higher-quality song.

■ The Sample Rate menu offers three choices—44.100 KHz (41,000 samples per second) is the standard number of samples for a CD-quality recording and 48.000 KHz is typical for recordings that are meant to be slightly better than CD-quality, or those that are compressed a bit more than CD audio. Or you can choose Auto to have iTunes choose for you.

TIP *Apple notes in its documentation for iTunes that there's no point in encoding a digital music file into another digital music file at a higher sample rate, because it won't improve quality. So if you're translating one digital music file into another format, choose the original's sample rate to get the best quality you can without bloating the file size.*

■ In the Channels menu, you can choose to encode in stereo or in mono. Mono saves space, but you probably don't want professionally recorded songs stored in mono if you can help it. Mono, however, is a more common format for audio books.

Once you've made your selections, click OK in the dialog box. You'll see the details area of the Importing settings in the iTunes Preferences window change to reflect your new settings.

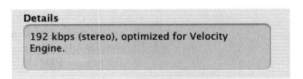

Details

192 kbps (stereo), optimized for Velocity Engine.

These are your new settings for encoding new audio (when importing from a CD) or for encoding an existing song when you choose Advanced | Convert Selection to AAC.

Encode in MP3

MP3 is popular for cross-platform playback, for use with stereo components, for playback in car stereos, and for portable digital music players. It is the de facto standard of digital music and, because music moves a bit slower then computing, it will probably remain the standard for at least a little while longer—Apple's foray into AAC notwithstanding. (The two can coexist, but we'll continue to hear about MP3s for some time to come.)

Even at this juncture, you may find it handy to switch Apple's default of creating AAC files back to MP3 for your own use, particularly if you have other equipment that can play back MP3 files. Plus, MP3 files are more flexible—settings run a wide gamut from song files that sound like AM radio (or even like a typical telephone connection) to songs that sound like crystal-clear CD quality. Fortunately, iTunes remains fully capable of encoding in MP3. To set it as your default, dig into the iTunes Preferences window, select Importing, and choose MP3 Encoded from the Import Using menu. When you do that, you can open the Settings menu and see that the MP3 Encoder offers three default bit rates—128 kbps, 160 kbps, and 192 kbps. Choose Custom, however, and you'll see the MP3 Encoder dialog box, which offers more choices than AAC:

- **Stereo Bit Rate**   Choose the kbps level for your connection. Somewhere in the 160 kbps range is considered very good, but you might want to set it higher for excellent playback sound and lower—even much lower—if you're trying to create small files.

- **Use Variable Bit Rate Encoding**   This option enables you to set a minimum bit rate—say, 128 kbps—but then allows the software to use a higher bit rate on complex parts of a song that would benefit from it. You can use the menu to tell iTunes what level of quality you're going for. The idea is to keep the quality level of the recording constant instead of the bit rate, which is allowed to vary somewhat over the baseline. The result is a slightly larger file for a more consistent level of quality.

NOTE   *Variable Bit Rate encoding works this way in iTunes, but not in all encoding products—some ask you to set a threshold and the bit rate can go above or below it. In iTunes, you set the lowest bit rate and the encoding may move up from there.*

- **Sample Rate** As with AAC, you can choose the number of samples per second that are used to represent the sound. The more samples, the closer the digital recording of the sound is to the original sound wave that was recorded. The MP3 encoder lets you go lower than the AAC encoder. You can drop all the way down to 8.000 KHz, which is about the audio quality of a telephone call. Auto uses the same rate at which an original song was encoded.

- **Channels** Choose stereo, mono (smaller file—about half the size), or auto, which converts mono tracks into mono MP3s and stereo tracks into stereo MP3s.

- **Stereo Mode** In normal mode, one track in the song carries the signal for the left stereo channel and one for the right. That makes sense. But for bit rates lower than 128 kbps, according to Apple, Joint Stereo mode—where one track carries data that's common to both the left and the right channel, while another track carries data that's unique for each channel—offers better playback within the bit rate constraints.

- **Smart Encoding Adjustments** Turn on this option to let iTunes take a whack at it, giving you a better quality song file by looking at the choices you've made and altering them where it seems to make sense.

- **Filter Frequencies Below 10 Hz** You can't hear frequencies that low (and even high-end subwoofers don't play frequencies that low), so tossing them out should lower the size of the file without affecting quality.

With all those choices made, click OK and you've set your standards for the MP3 files that you decide to encode by either importing audio from CDs or by selecting a song in your library and choosing Advanced | Convert Selection to MP3. What you've got is a fairly sophisticated MP3 translator at your disposal.

Encode in AIFF

The next format that iTunes is capable of encoding to is AIFF, Audio Interchange File Format, which has been the standard for audio files on the Macintosh for many years. AIFF began its life as an uncompressed format, and the compression approaches that have come along since then are less sophisticated than those you'll find in MP3 or AAC. As a practical format for music and digital audio playback, AIFF leaves something to be desired, as the files it creates are pretty big. (In a little experiment I just conducted in iTunes, a high-quality, four-minute AAC that I have in my library is 3.9MB in size; translated to AIFF, it takes up 42MB on the disk. Ouch.) That's because AIFF audio isn't compressed much (sometimes not at all) compared to AAC and MP3 audio formats.

It's a great format, however, if you want to edit that audio and you have a Macintosh. (That is, *particularly* if you have a Macintosh—although a lot of Windows applications can handle AIFF files without trouble.) If you've got other applications that you want to use for editing songs that you pull off of your CDs—or if you want to translate MP3s or AAC audio files for use in editing programs, you may find that AIFF is more universally accepted than those other formats.

To set iTunes up to encode AIFF, open iTunes Preferences and click the Importing button. In the Import Using menu, choose AIFF Encoder. Next, choose Custom from the Setting menu—and up comes the AIFF Encoder dialog box, which is pretty dull, with just three settings:

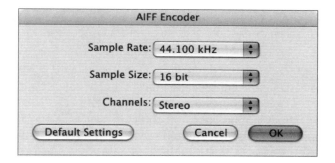

And those settings are

- **Sample Rate**   Choose the rate, remembering that 44.100 KHz is CD-quality, 22.050 is about FM radio quality, and 11.025 approximates AM radio.

- **Sample Size**   This one is different from MP3 and AAC, but standard for older audio formats. Years back, computer audio was all 8-bit, meaning, essentially, each sample must be represented as one of 256 tones, whereas with 16-bit audio, you have 65,536 possible tones, which means 16-bit is much more likely to be accurate—but the file is larger. These days, any high-quality AIFF worth hearing is 16-bit. (Eight-bit should be left for little two-second sound samples that you use to make your computer's alert sound cutesy.)

■ **Channels**   Choose Mono to use less storage space, Stereo if you want to maintain the fidelity of an existing stereo sample, and Auto if you want iTunes to make the decision for you.

Those are the choices. Click OK if you're ready to start encoding in AIFF. That's what you'll get when you import from a CD or select a file and then choose Advanced | Convert Selection To AIFF.

Here's a little trick. The Macintosh sees audio CD tracks as AIFF files, so you can insert an audio CD and, once it's mounted, access it in the Finder. Drag a song from the audio CD to your hard disk and the AIFF file is saved.

Encode in WAV

Our final option is the WAV format, the de facto standard for years on the Windows platform because it was built into Windows 95 and was part of the introduction of digital audio to the mainstream of PC users. WAV is the mirror image of AIFF in the sense that it's most often used for editing these days, particularly given the popularity of MP3 for playback and transporting digital music files and the relative lack of support (or, at least, a lack of momentum) for the AAC format in Windows.

So, while iTunes may not be your first choice for encoding WAV files, it can be handy if you want to translate something that you've got for use in a music editor on a PC. (And, having this ability in iTunes on a Mac means never asking yourself—how can I play and/or translate to and from a WAV file?) Again, file sizes are huge—my four-minute sample song (4MB as an AAC) is 42MB, just like AIFF, since both are uncompressed formats.

To set iTunes up to encode WAV, open iTunes Preferences and click the Importing button. In the Import Using menu, choose WAV Encoder. Next, choose Custom from the Setting menu. You'll now encounter the WAV Encoder dialog box, which is pretty dull, with just three settings that are identical to those discussed in the previous section on encoding AIFF files: Sample Rate, Sample Size, and Channels. Make your choices and click OK. When you do, you're set to encode imported songs as WAV, whether they're imported from a CD, dragged in from a disk, or translated using the Advanced | Convert Selection To WAV.

Edit Digital Audio Files

Want to get more creative with your music files? Perhaps you want to create your own. Or perhaps you just want to mix and mess with the songs you've already got. If that's the case, you may have already seen, in the previous section of this chapter, one of the keys—iTunes can act as a translation platform for audio recorded in AIFF or WAV, which are common formats for creating and editing audio in Mac OS X and in Microsoft Windows, respectively. So, if you'd like to turn a recording into an MP3 or an AAC file, you can record it first in AIFF or WAV, which your editing software is likely to be familiar with. Then, if your editing software doesn't translate to MP3 or AAC, you can use iTunes to do it. This transaction can also go in the opposite direction—from MP3 or AAC to AIFF or WAV using iTunes, which will then enable you to edit the audio file.

> NOTE   *Realize that translating from a compressed format—MP3 to AAC—to an uncompressed format and then editing the song is less ideal than beginning with an uncompressed format, making your edits and then encoding into a compressed format. If you encode a compressed format (say, MP3) into another compressed format (say AAC), you experience a little generation loss, as compressed bits get subjected again to a different compressor. Likewise, if you went, for instance, from MP3 to AIFF to AAC, you'd experience some quality loss.*

9

Why would you want to edit? You may have your own reasons. Perhaps you want to add your own singing to a song that you have stored as an MP3 in order to create a duet (oh, wait, that's *me*), or you play a mean guitar and want to add that to some piano recordings you've got. Some sound software is designed to sweeten—or distort—recorded audio, and you may find that sort of thing pleasing. Professional audio software (and software for serious hobbyists) can offer all sorts of filters and fun stuff like that. And, of course, you may want to begin with an original recording—whether it's a song, a poem, or a recorded speech—and turn that into an MP3 or similar digital audio file. You can do it with iTunes.

The key begins with making sure that you're working with an audio file that's in the format you need it to be in—from there, the trick is just to have the right software to help you make the edits.

Edit Sound Files on a Mac

A number of professional editing applications exist for the Macintosh, which is popular among the pros for audio editing and music creation. Bias, Inc. (www.bias-inc.com) offers a gamut of interesting audio editing applications for Macintosh, including Bias Deck, a multitrack editor that's good for producing bands or movie soundtracks; Bias Peak and Peak LE (see Figure 9-5), which offer sophisticated waveform editing; and SoundSoap, a unique application for dealing with analog noise in your digital recordings (see the upcoming "How to" sidebar).

i3 Software Engineering offers DSP-Quattro (www.dsp-quattro.com), a sound editing application aimed at not just digital audio files, but also digital music synthesis and MIDI control. In other words, it's a tad complex, but relatively affordable (99 Euros—it's an Italian company).

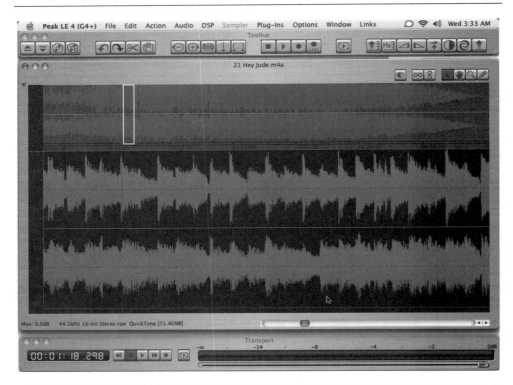

FIGURE 9-5   Peak LE is the low-cost version of the popular commercial audio editing application.

One of my favorites is also among the least expensive: Sound Studio. Sound Studio, from Felt Tip software (www.felttip.com), is a wonderful offering with a 14-day demo available from the web site. It's straightforward, easy to understand, and it works with the file formats we've discussed in this chapter, including both AIFF and WAV. It can also export to MP3 or AAC.

One of the main reasons I find myself working in an application such as Sound Studio is to edit songs so that I can use them in an application like iMovie as the sound track for the videos that I edit. Working in Sound Studio is a little handier than working in iMovie because of iMovie's limited audio controls. In Sound Studio, the precise control allows for audio files that do exactly what I want them to do, and which last as long as I want them to play.

Plus, Sound Studio offers a number of fun filters that—once you get to know them—can be handy friends in your quest for better sounding songs and digital audio. Also, for people who love the sound of your own voice (we know who we are), even a simpler audio editing application like Sound Studio can be used to record speaking or singing and then later overlaid with other audio. Afterward, it could be exported in a file format that could then be used in iTunes. The most obvious application for such technology is radio plays that you produce at home. (In fact, if your radio play is good enough, you might even be able to make some money off it. I know people who make thousands of dollars selling "electronic books," after all. Boy, that Internet sure is the darnedest thing.)

We can't get deep into how to actually accomplish things in Sound Studio, but it's worth taking a look at. Check out Figure 9-6, which shows Sound Studio in action. I've used the File | Import Using QuickTime to import an AAC file into the application and then saved it as an AIFF for editing. (It would have been better to import the song as an AIFF in the first place, to maintain the best quality, but the fact that Sound Studio can manage this is pretty cool.) What we see are the waveforms for each channel—left (L) and right (R)—of the music file.

Once the audio is in the application, what can be done with it is fascinating. First, you can move it around, or chop it off. If I've got a video clip that only lasts one minute and I've got a four-minute song, I might dig into the song and find a good place that lasts about one minute and then use it in the video. (It won't always be the very beginning of the song, since I may want the song to begin abruptly to set the mood.) By selecting that one minute (you can choose Edit | Set Selection to choose the exact selection using minutes and seconds) and choosing Edit | Crop, you can get rid of all the excess and focus only on that selection for editing. (Once you crop it, you might consider using the File | Save As command to give the cropped portion a different name so you can revert to the original file if you change your mind about the section you want to use.)

9

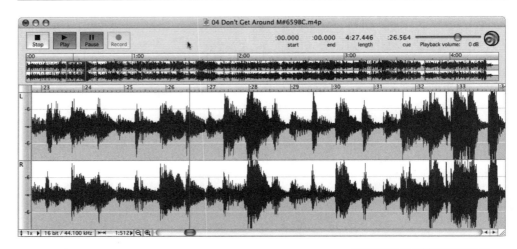

FIGURE 9-6   Here's a song imported into Sound Studio.

Once you've got the portion of audio you want, there's tons of stuff you can do with it. Cut and Paste works great in Sound Studio. Select a portion of your song and choose Edit | Copy or Edit | Cut, then move to another area and choose Edit | Paste Inserting (to add the portion that you've cut or copied into the song) or Edit | Paste Mixing (to mix the clip that you've cut or copied with the original audio, adding the two together). As you can see, the flexibility makes it great for something like audio for digital video, but it can be useful for adding your singing vocals to a recording melody line or something along those lines. (Producing a whole band would be quite a task in Sound Studio—one best left for Bias Deck or a similar application, but mixing together a few different tracks isn't a big problem.)

> **TIP** *Want to record yourself? You can see the Input Levels window that appears when you're working in Sound Studio. It's telling you whether or not it can hear any audio input, perhaps through your Mac's built-in or attached microphone, and it shows you the levels that it's hearing. To record something, select an open area in your audio file or choose File | New to create a new audio file. Then, just click Record in the Sound Studio window for that audio file and start singing or speaking or whatever it is that you want to do. When you click stop or press ⌘-. (period), the recording stops and you can play back what you've recorded.*

Other fun and games happen when you opt to use a filter on your audio. The filters can get a little complex, but once you start reading a little about editing and improving audio, you'll find that it's nice to have some of the filters that Sound Studio offers. Some filters are easy to grasp, like Filter | Fade Out, which will slowly lower the volume in a linear way along a selection in your song. This is a great way to end it, particularly if you've cropped the song down to its middle. Beyond Fade Out is Filter | Fade Special, which enables you to shape the way that the audio selection will fade out:

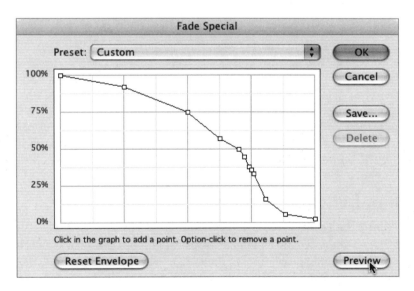

Other filters include Normalize (which attempts to fix any volume extremes in the audio file), DC Offset (which removes sounds below the threshold of hearing),

Backward (which enables you to play the song backward), Chorus, Echo, and Reverb settings (which can add some richness to the sound by simulating different circumstances, such as large concert halls), and many others.

When you've done all the editing and filtering that you've set out to do, you're ready to save the file. You have two choices—you can save the file as an AIFF or WAV (whichever you're editing in) and then use iTunes to encode it as an MP3 or AAC, if that's your desire. Or, you can use Sound Studio's ability to export using QuickTime's filter, which enables you to save the file in its current format, but gives you more control over the settings. Choose File | Export With QuickTime and you'll see a dialog box that may look familiar—it's similar to the dialog boxes you see when setting up encoding in iTunes.

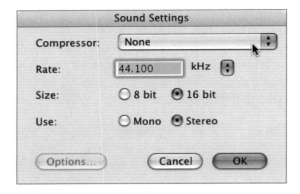

If you're working with an AIFF file and you opt to export and choose a Compressor, then you'll save the file as an AIFF-C, which is the compressed version of AIFF. If you don't choose a Compressor, then you'll save the file as a straight AIFF, which you can then import into iTunes and encode as you please.

Edit Sound Files in Windows

Windows offers both professional and consumer sound editing software as well, including Sony's SoundForge (mediasoftware.sonypictures.com), which is very popular for professional applications; Steinberg's WaveLab (www.steinbergusa.net); and Adobe Audition, formerly Cool Edit, which is a popular package for professional level mixing, recording, and file translation.

Of course, plenty of sound editing shareware can be had for Windows. One standout is Audacity, a very basic editor for Windows (actually, it's cross-platform, supporting Mac OS X as well) that is a popular download because it works with WAV, AIFF, and MP3 files, enabling you to edit them, mix tracks together, and apply effects to the music. Audacity is extensible with plug-ins that add features and capabilities, and it's free since it's distributed as open source software.

> **TIP** *One tip I happened to read on the Audacity web site is worth sharing. With a program like Audacity, you can sometimes remove the vocals from a song if it was recorded in such a way that the vocals are "centered" on the left and right tracks, with the instruments off-center. If you subtract the right channel from the left channel (something you can do in Audacity and many other editors), you may end up with the instruments without the vocal (or with much less vocal).*

Audacity doesn't ship with an MP3 or AAC encoder, but that makes it a good companion for iTunes, which can take the WAV files you create in Audacity and encode them easily, as was discussed earlier. (Audacity can also download a freeware encoder and use it.)

Another shareware option I like for Windows is Acoustica, from Acon Digital Media (www.acondigital.com). Acoustica is more advanced than Audacity, but it's aimed directly at users who want to edit and transform digital music files. Along with the usual suspects, such as track editing tools, filters, and effects, Acoustica offers built-in tools that allow on-the-fly channel mixing (for creating karaoke tracks or otherwise playing with the stereo mix of your music files) and other high-end features, which are a real bargain given Acoustica's $29 price tag (at the time of this writing).

Of course, many other editors abound. Whereas Mac OS X often has two or three good shareware and freeware applications for a given purpose, Windows will often have at least five to ten good applications—and scores more that are mediocre, or less feature-rich, but still available to play with. Visit a site like download.com.com to browse through the available titles for either a Mac or PC.

9

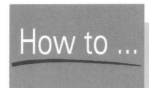

Translate Analog Recordings to Digital

Many people with an interest in digital audio will eventually find themselves interested in transferring analog music—from their vinyl record collection or from cassettes or other stereo components (hopefully not from eight-tracks)— to their computer for storage for use as a digital music file. Actually, this is usually pretty easy to accomplish once you get your stereo hooked up to your computer and some form of recording software (including most of the packages discussed in this section).

To connect an analog turntable or cassette player to your computer, the best plan is to run a line-level output from your stereo system's receiver to your computer's line-level input. You'll generally need a Y-adapter that connects RCA-style plugs for the audio out on the receiver to the mini-plug adapter that's used on the back (or side) of your computer. You don't want to use speaker outputs from the receiver, and you probably want to avoid the headphone jack—the line-level inputs are best, as they allow you more control over volume and potential distortion.

Next, you'll need something that can record the audio. One solution is to use an audio editor, such as Audacity (discussed earlier in this section) to record to an AIFF or WAV file that can then be encoded to MP3 or AAC using iTunes. In fact, recording the analog audio is easy. The hard part is turning an LP into a series of individual songs that can each be saved and encoded as digital music files. That's why the best trick is to use software that's specifically designed for dealing with LPs. For Windows, CFB Software (www.cfbsoftware.com) makes LP Recorder and LP Ripper, which help automate the process of recording analog audio and turning it into individual "tracks" that can be used for creating digital music files and/or burning them to audio CDs. LP Recorder also includes technology to quiet hisses and manage gaps between songs.

Macs have options that include some programs that aren't 100 percent aimed at recording LPs and cassettes, but that still work, such as BlackCat's AudioCorder (www.blackcatsystems.com/software/audiocorder.html) and Sound Studio. The easiest solution is a commercial application such as Roxio's Jam (www.roxio .com), which works in conjunction with Toast (get it?) to arrange tracks and build a CD from audio files.

Chapter 10

Mac Issues, Windows Issues

How to...

- ■ Record Web Radio on a Mac
- ■ Record Web Radio in Windows
- ■ Use AppleScripts for iTunes
- ■ Use MP3s and Windows Media
- ■ Use iTunes and iMovie

It's actually pretty amazing how similar iTunes for Macintosh and iTunes for Windows are. This is true in both iTunes' look and feel, and even in much of the underlying technology thanks to the presence of QuickTime in both cases. In fact, the applications are so alike that the only real differences to talk about on the surface show up in some of the dialog boxes that they rely on their respective operating systems for, such as the Open and Save dialog boxes.

That said, the truth is that iTunes for Macintosh is a more mature product than iTunes for Windows, since the Mac version has been out for a number of years now. Furthermore, iTunes for Mac does have some hidden capabilities based on Apple-specific technology. Apple knows its own operating system pretty well, so when it built iTunes, it included hooks for technology like AppleScript, which enables you to automatically run iTunes with scripts or incorporate it into small programs that allow iTunes to work with other Mac applications. (Even cooler is the option of finding and downloading other people's scripts, particularly if you aren't much of a programmer yourself.)

In this chapter, we'll also talk about something that's fairly platform-specific—the ability to record audio from iTunes radio. This can be handy if you'd like to gain access to something you heard on an Internet radio station that you'd like to save on your computer for posterity. This not only includes music, but also Internet talk shows, business conference calls, product demos—anything that is done using audio streaming technology.

Finally, we'll take a look at two different technologies worth discussing in the context of iTunes—Apple's iMovie digital-video editing software and Microsoft's Windows Media. Both are items you don't have to know anything about to enjoy iTunes, but incorporating them into your understanding may make your digital audio experience that much richer. In fact, it could change your life. (But probably not.)

Record Audio Streams

In order to record audio streams—Web radio, live streams, and so on—you need special applications. The applications are able to intercept the signal as its downloaded and, on the fly, create an MP3 file from that signal. That means you can record and archive all sorts of recordings. It also means you need software that's specific to the computer platform that you're using, whether it's Windows or Mac.

> **NOTE**   *You should consider the copyright infringement implications of recording commercial audio that you haven't paid for. Remember that the artist suffers when you don't pay for music.*

Mac-Based Recording

Let's start with a quick look at some software that you can use to record streaming audio onto your Mac. One popular option is called StreamRipperX (see Figure 10-1), which sounds a bit violent, but it's meant to suggest that you can "rip" (sort of slang for import-to-MP3) an audio stream on Mac OS X. The application's home page is streamripperx.sourceforge.net, and its free software is released under the GNU General Public License.

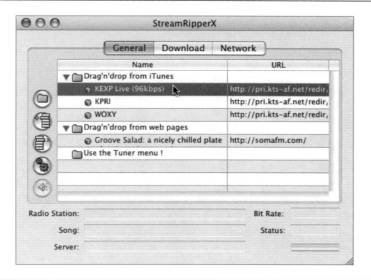

FIGURE 10-1   StreamRipperX can be used to record audio streams.

StreamRipperX plays very well with iTunes. It works well with iTunes Radio or with any streams that you've added in other ways (by clicking links to them on web pages or dragging those links to iTunes, for instance). To add a stream to StreamRipperX, simply drag it from iTunes to the folder marked "Drag'n'drop from iTunes" or drag a URL from your browser to the folder marked "Drag'n'drop from web pages."

With streams added, in StreamRipperX, select a stream and choose Streams | Listen with iTunes (or ⌘-L) to hear that particular stream played through iTunes. Now, as you're listening, you can make the decision to record the stream by clicking the record button in StreamRipperX. It's the small button that looks like the gears in a machine:

Doing so begins the recording process. You'll see, under the name of the stream, the name of the recording that's being created. With some MP3 streams, you'll simply see the stream's name and it will record continuously—just as if you had plugged a cassette recorder into your stereo and were recording a local radio station.

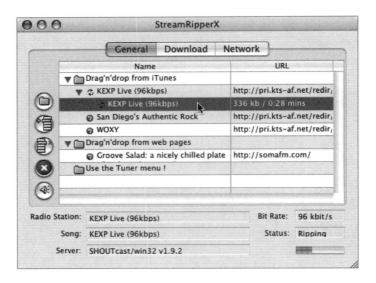

In other cases, you may see the name of an MP3 file appear below the stream's name. This indicates that the stream you're listening to also sends along MP3

information that enables StreamRipperX to rip each individual song as an MP3 file, which can certainly be handy for use in iTunes. To stop the recording, click the "X" button (it's what the "gears" button has become).

The streams that you record in StreamRipperX are stored in your personal music file by default, although you can change this by selecting the Download tab in the window and entering a different path for your downloads. When you're ready to play your songs, open that download folder (again, by default it's the Music folder inside your home folder) and either double-click the recorded MP3 you want to hear or drag one or more of the MP3s to your iTunes Library so it can be added to your collection.

 *Want to delete items in StreamRipperX? Select a stream, a station, or a recording and click the Delete button, which has a small "x" as part of its icon. You can also choose Streams | Delete or press ⌘-D.*

Another option for recording audio streams on the Mac is actually another option for nearly everything that iTunes does. It's called Audion and hails from a great software company called Panic Software that creates high-quality Mac applications. Audion is really aimed at being an iTunes killer, if that's possible, and is loaded with capabilities such as CD playback, MP3 encoding, and even streaming to a Streamcast server. Since it doesn't work directly with iTunes, it's a little outside the scope of this book, but you'll find more information about it at www.panic.com/audion on the Web.

A third neat little freeware program is WireTap from Ambrosia (www.ambrosiasw .com/utilities/freebies), which enables you to record *any* audio that you're Mac is playing, including iTunes songs or pretty much anything else, including even audio chats in iChat AV. Plus, it's got a little window that you use for controlling the recording:

Record Streams in Windows

Given iTunes for Windows' newness, there currently aren't any stream recorders specifically designed for iTunes the way they are in the Mac world (or at least at the time of this writing there weren't). However, you'll still find you can accomplish the task of recording MP3 streams from within Windows. You may just have to jump through an extra hoop or two.

One option is called, cleverly enough, StreamRipper32, and it's available from http://streamripper.sourceforge.net on the Web. While it doesn't work directly with iTunes (you can't simply play a stream in iTunes and record it directly in the program), it does work directly with streaming MP3 URLs—so, if you locate a direct address for an MP3 stream, you can enter it in the Server address area (see Figure 10-2) and then begin to record that stream.

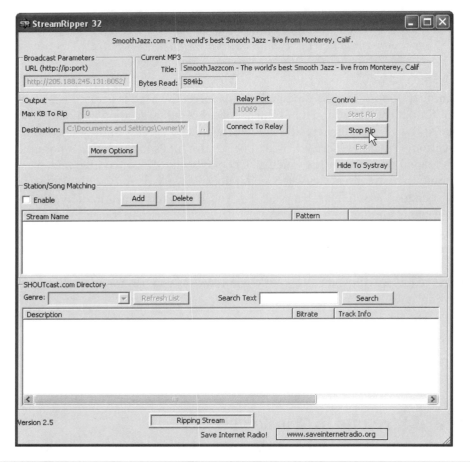

FIGURE 10-2   The StreamRipper32 window enables you to enter a URL and then access that stream for recording.

To record the stream, first choose a file name (click the small "." icon on the right side of the Destination entry box and use the Save dialog box to choose where the file will be saved), then enter the URL in the URL entry box and click the Start Rip button. When you're done, you'll have an MP3 file (or a series of MP3 files, if StreamRipper32 is able to split the stream into songs) that you can locate on your hard disk and then drag into the iTune's Library in order to play it back and otherwise work with that recording.

This brings us to the issue of how to get URLs from the streams that you've located from within iTunes. Actually, it can be done—although it doesn't always work, depending on the complexity of the URL—here's how:

■ Find the stream that you want to record and select it in iTunes. If the stream is not in your library or playlist (if it's in the Radio listings, for instance), then you need to drag that listing to your library or a playlist first.

■ With the stream selected, choose File | Get Info.

■ In the Information window, make sure the Summary tab is selected.

■ Click the Edit URL entry box.

■ Highlight the URL and choose CTRL-C to copy it.

■ Switch to StreamRipper (or whatever program you're using), highlight the URL entry box, and press CTRL-V to paste the URL into it.

That's all it takes. Note that this doesn't work for all URLs with StreamRipper. ShoutCast streams and simpler URLs are better and sometimes the server won't allow StreamRipper to access it.

Another option is called RipCast, and it's similar in purpose to StreamRipperX discussed in the previous section. RipCast enables you to "rip" MP3s directly from streaming audio. If the streaming audio has ID3 information embedded in it, then the MP3s can be saved as individual files; if not, the stream is recorded as one large MP3 that you can play back or edit. RipCast can be downloaded from www.xoteck .xom/ripcast/ on the Web.

Once installed, you begin by launching RipCast, which acts not only as an MP3 ripper, but also as a stream browser, enabling you to find the streams you want to record (see Figure 10-3). When you launch a station's URL or playlist, you'll see the RipCast Agent window appear, which enables you to rip music from that station.

10

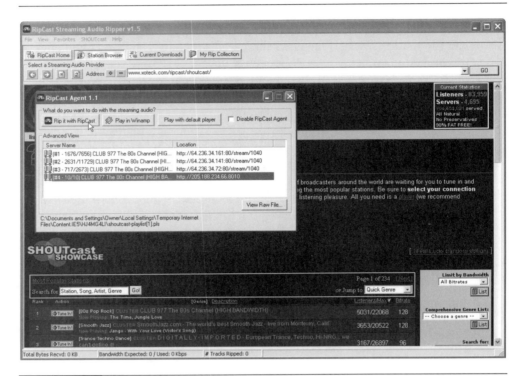

FIGURE 10-3   RipCast is a full-fledged application for browsing (in the background) and recording (foreground) online MP3 streams.

NOTE *Visit my site for this book at www.mac-upgrade.com/itunes for updates regarding Windows software, as I wrote this book in the first few days of the Windows version of iTunes' availability. As time wears on and iTunes proves its popularity, you'll likely see more shareware and open source tools designed specifically to work with iTunes, and I'll keep track of those online.*

AppleScript Automation for iTunes for Mac

The Mac's AppleScript technology (which enables the knowledgeable user to create scripts that can automate Mac applications) has its hooks into iTunes. In fact, a great deal of what iTunes does can be scripted by those who know a little something about AppleScript. And, fortunately, those people like to go public with their scripts and offer them to the rest of us so that those of us who *aren't* terribly knowledgeable about scripting can take advantage of their expertise. In this section, we'll take a look at some of those scripts, where you'll find them and how to use them. Then we'll take a quick look at the AppleScript dictionary for iTunes so you can dig further into scripting iTunes on your own if it interests you.

Apple's AppleScripts for iTunes

The first place to start looking for AppleScripts is at the mothership's web site—www.apple.com/applescript/itunes. There they've posted two sets of scripts (at the time of writing) for iTunes versions that work in the classic Mac OS and in Mac OS X. Since the latest version of iTunes works in Mac OS X only (and Apple hasn't updated this page in a while since I last looked), it's the second bundle that's more interesting for our purposes. The stuff this bundle can do is pretty cool, including scripts that work with the CDDB database to look up songs and artists, scripts that automate the creation of playlists (you can create a playlist that includes all of the songs of a certain artist that are in your database, for instance), and scripts that look up selected songs, albums, or artists in popular online music services like CDNOW and eMusic. (You'd think Apple might do away with those scripts now that they have the iTunes Music Store.) One script enables you to toggle the check mark for every highlighted track, another generates a text file that summarizes the contents of your library, and another one enables you to set a portion of a single song track to loop repeatedly. Still others do handy things like purge your library of songs that don't have a file associated with them or search and replace parts of the names of every song in your library. There's more, too.

To install these scripts, drag the iTunes folder out of the archive's folder and into the library folder on your Mac's startup disk. If you don't have administrator privileges or if you don't want to make these scripts available to everyone on this Mac, you can drag the iTunes folder to the library folder inside your Mac instead. Once you do that, you'll see an AppleScript menu appear on your Mac's menu bar (see Figure 10-4).

Once the scripts are installed, you're ready to work with them. With most of the scripts, you'll begin by highlighting a particular song or track (or multiple tracks) in iTunes and then you'll select the script you want to run from the Script menu (also see Figure 10-4).

With a few of the scripts, what's selected isn't important—such as "Play Random Track" or the script "Set Genre to Specific EQ." In the first case, you'll just see a dialog box appear that tells you about the new random track that's being played.

10

FIGURE 10-4 Activating an Applescript script in iTunes

In the second case, a window will pop up, asking you for further feedback (in this case, you're choosing the genre in question). This second script's window is shown in Figure 10-5.

Other AppleScripts for iTunes

Of course, Apple isn't the only place you can uncover AppleScripts for iTunes. You'll also find them at Doug's AppleScripts for iTunes (www.malcolmadams.com/itunes/index.shtml), which is probably the most important bookmark for anyone interested in both AppleScript and iTunes. The site offers a repository of hundreds of scripts submitted from across the Web, which have now been made available for download.

Scripts on the site are organized into scripts that manage tracks, manage track info, work with playlists, control iTunes, export information from your songs, manage your underlying files, deal with your iPod, and help iTunes work with

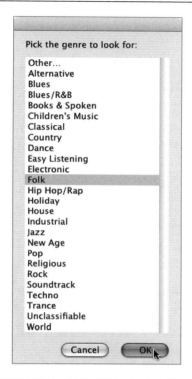

FIGURE 10-5   The window that appears when you choose the "Set Genre to Specific EQ" script.

other applications. As of this writing, there are just under 250 scripts and they can do all kinds of things. Some of my favorite examples include:

- **Wrangle Same-Named Tracks**   Tracks with the same name will all be placed in a new playlist so you can decide if the tracks are duplicates or if any of them need to be renamed.

- **Downstream**   Removes radio stations from your main library and places them in a playlist.

- **Legitimize Song**   Allows you to select an MP3 (or a series of them) and automatically have them replaced with newly purchased AAC files from the iTunes Music Store.

- **Artwork Scripts**   Enables you to assign existing artwork to all of the songs from a particular album.

- **Composer-ize/Genre-ize**   Two scripts that enable you to change the entries in these fields to text that makes more sense or that you think is more appropriate.

- **iTunes Music Store Player**   Allows you to select more than one song at a time in the iTunes Music Store and have each play sequentially. This is handy since you're typically required to click each song manually to hear it.

- **iTunes DJ**   This script switches between Internet radio stations at intervals that you specify, and will even introduce the stations and make (according to their description) snide remarks.

- **Quick Convert**   Enables you to select and convert tracks (to MP3, AAC, AIFF, or WAV) without forcing you to first go into iTunes Preferences and change the Importing settings.

- **Audiobooker**   This script takes audio books from CD (or multiple CDs) and imports them with intelligently ordered tracks and so on.

- **Rip This Where I Want It**   Enables you to import a CD track and place it, not in the iTunes Library folder, but in whatever folder you wish.

- **Google Lyrics Search**   Select a song and then search for that song's lyrics in Google.

You get the idea. There are tons of these scripts that you can page through and look to see if any of them answer your specific needs. I haven't even mentioned some of the most fun scripts, such as those that work with other applications, including iTunes2Mail or Now Playing in iChat AV, which automatically puts the name of the song you're listening to in your Mail signature when you send a message to someone. Shown here is the iChat AV (Apple's Internet chat and videoconferencing application) displaying the song that I'm currently listening to, and which can be seen by my iChat "buddies":

To add scripts to iTunes, you can do one of two things. If you'd like the scripts to appear to any user of your Mac who launched iTunes, you need to put them in the main library folder. (You also need to be working in an account with administrator's permissions if you want to do this.) If there isn't already an iTunes folder in that library folder, create one. Next, create a subfolder inside that iTunes folder called Scripts. Now, copy the script that you've downloaded to that Scripts folder.

If you want the script to only be available to you when you're working in your own account on this Mac, then you need to work with the library folder that's in your home folder. Open your home folder, and then open the library folder. You've likely got an iTunes folder—open it and create a Scripts folder inside it if you don't see one. Now, drag the script file to that Scripts folder (see Figure 10-6).

TIP   *Want to post your iTunes Library on the Web to tell folks what you listen to? Doug's AppleScripts for iTunes offers a few scripts such as "Playlist to HTML" and "Export as HTML Table." If you have access to server-side scripting, check out the script phptunetest (www.maczsoftware.com/phptunest), which enables you to use the built-in iTunes function to export your iTunes Library as an XML file (File | Export Library In iTunes) and then post that file on your web site. When you do, the script will automatically generate an HTML-table results pages on your web site that displays all your songs and iTunes tracks.*

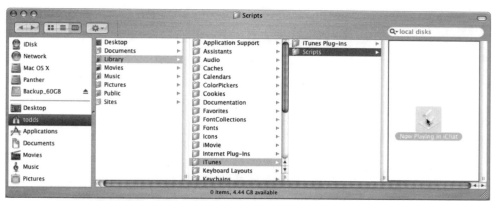

FIGURE 10-6   Dragging a script to the Scripts folder inside the iTunes folder inside the library folder inside my home folder. (Whew!)

iTunes' AppleScript Dictionary

Know a little something about AppleScript? If you don't, then you might want to hang around at Doug's AppleScripts for iTunes web site (discussed in the previous section) where you can get hints and tips about scripting in the discussion forums. For a more formal introduction, try Apple's AppleScript site at www.apple.com/applescript. A primer on AppleScript is a little outside the scope of this book.

What I would like to point out, however, is that iTunes is incredibly scriptable, and includes a full accounting of the items and commands that it can respond to in its AppleScript dictionary. Any Mac application that responds to more than the very basic AppleScript commands has a dictionary, and iTunes is no exception.

To view the dictionary, first launch the AppleScript Script Editor, which is located in the AppleScript folder inside your main Applications folder. Next, choose File | Open Dictionary. In the open dialog box, locate and select iTunes (you're looking at a list of scriptable applications) and click Open. When you do, you'll see the iTunes dictionary, shown in Figure 10-7.

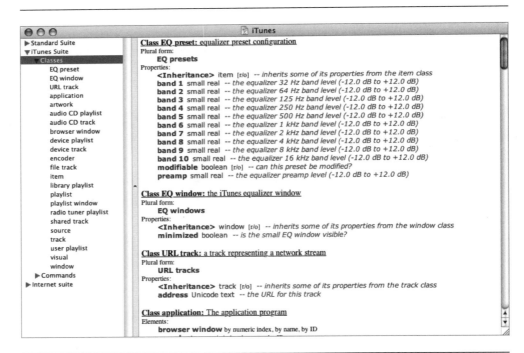

FIGURE 10-7 The iTunes dictionary shows you the special objects and commands that can be used for scripting iTunes.

To view items in the dictionary, select a suite on the left-hand side and then choose whether you want to view classes (the items that can have something done to them) or commands (the tasks that AppleScript can do.) Scroll through and you'll see not only the items that can be altered but also the settings and the options for altering them—these are the building blocks of an AppleScript.

When you're done viewing the iTunes dictionary, click its Close button or choose File | Close to close the window.

MP3 and Windows Media

iTunes for Windows, as of its debut version, doesn't offer much in the way of hidden Windows-only features, and it doesn't support AppleScript. What is worth talking about in this section, though, is the interaction that you're likely to encounter with Windows Media Player which, in Windows, is sort of a combination of iTunes and QuickTime Player on the Mac. Windows Media Player can play back all sorts of audio and video content, including CDs, local files, Internet streams, and other content. It's meant as the central multimedia application in Windows (particularly Windows XP), so you'll probably encounter it before long.

When you installed iTunes, it actually asks you if you want it to take over some of the duties assigned to Windows Media Player—for instance, the playback of audio CDs that you insert in your PC. When you insert a CD without iTunes running, however, you'll likely see a dialog box that looks something like this:

Using this dialog box, you can choose to play the CD in iTunes or in other applications, including the Windows Media Player. You can also choose to immediately copy music from the CD to Windows Media Player. When you make your choice, that application will launch and begin to manage the CD. If your choice is the Windows Media Player, then you'll see something that looks like Figure 10-8.

The Windows Media Player, by default, uses a default digital music format that we haven't really discussed at all in this book, called WMA (Windows Media Audio). The format is similar to MP3 but offers better compression and it's not directly compatible with MP3 players and applications that don't specifically support WMA.

So, what Windows Media Player represents is something that's quintessentially Microsoft—a propriety format that works pretty well and that will likely be supported by a majority of digital music applications and hardware in the future because it's Microsoft's format and Microsoft is dominant in the industry. While MP3 is an industry standard, Windows discourages its use with the Windows Media Player, encouraging Windows users, instead, to stick with Microsoft's "brand" of digital music file. And that "brand" is incompatible with generic players and applications.

FIGURE 10-8   The Windows Media Player with a CD's songs being imported.

Interestingly, Apple is playing a similar, although not identical game. By choosing AAC for its default format (both for burning CDs and for selling digital music tracks), Apple has made its music incompatible with the majority of digital music devices as well, and applications are catching up to support the AAC format, even for simple translation to and from MP3. Apple makes that easy by offering QuickTime technology on the Mac and in Windows, which application developers can access for their programming. Likewise, AAC is technically an open standard, unlike WMA. Also, it so happens that, as of this writing, Apple dominates the digital music hardware market with the iPod, garnering a large enough market share that it may be able to push the AAC format into wider acceptance.

This long-winded explanation is meant to make two things clear. First, if you use Windows Media Player to copy songs from your CDs, you'll need to continue to use Windows Media Player for both playback and for the management of those songs, including CD burning. iTunes isn't an option, because it doesn't support the WMA format. If you did want to play those songs, you'd first need to convert them from WMA to MP3 using a converter application that can handle WMA. (A CD burned out of the Windows Media Player is still a standard audio CD, however, so you could conceivably use that CD for importing songs.)

Second, if you plan to use an iPod or an MP3 player that doesn't support WMA, you might want to stick with iTunes for updating that device since it's good both for devices that support AAC and those that support MP3. Plus, with the exception of songs bought from the iTunes Music Store, it's a simple matter to convert AAC songs to MP3 and then place them on your third-party MP3 playback device.

Having said all that, the Windows Media Player is still tons of fun for playing back audio CDs, video clips, and tuning in radio formats that are Windows Media friendly. (Be sure to check out the "skins" which can turn the Windows Media Player application into some funky looking shapes and images, too.) Just remember that the stuff you save or encode using Windows Media Player will likely need a little translation before it can be used with iTunes, the iPod, or, for that matter, pretty much anything else that doesn't have the Windows Media Player seal of approval.

iTunes and iMovie

As with all of Apple's "iApps," iTunes and iMovie have a special relationship. iMovie is Apple's digital video-editing software. It enables you to connect a digital video camcorder to your Mac, download the video from that camcorder to your computer and then edit the video images into a "movie"—whether it's a home video, business video, documentary, or—if you're the creative type—a feature film. Using iMovie, you add transitions, titles, special effects, and, of course, audio and music.

The relationship that iTunes has to iMovie is one that you might be able to guess—you can use songs from the iTunes Library as a soundtrack for your iMovie videos. In fact, iMovie makes it easy for you to access your iTunes Library directly from within iMovie, which is pretty darned convenient.

Accessing the iTunes Library from within iMovie is simple. In iMovie, select the Audio button in the effects pane. The pane will change to show audio options. If you don't already see it, choose iTunes Library from the menu at the top of the pane. Now you'll see your library of songs (see Figure 10-9).

You can select individual playlists from the menu at the top of the pane, just below the iTunes Library entry. You might want to organize your songs in iTunes first so that you can quickly access the songs you think might be appropriate for your movie's soundtrack.

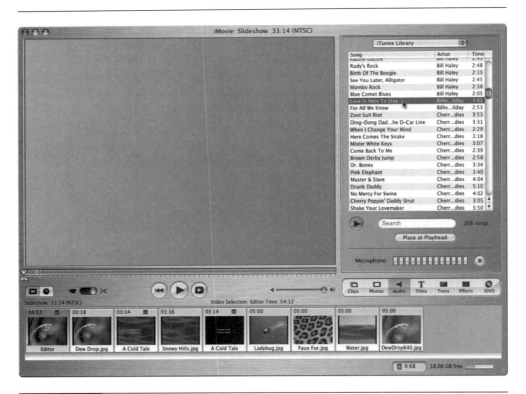

FIGURE 10-9 In iMovie, you can directly access the iTunes Library to add songs to the videos that you edit.

Select a song and you can click the Play button (the right-facing arrow) to hear the song playback. (You can also double-click a song to play it.)

Once you've selected the song you want to use, click the Place At Playhead button and the song will appear on the iMovie timeline at the playhead.

Note that you can also drag a song from the listing in the Audio pane down to the timeline. When you drop it, the song is placed pretty much as if you'd clicked the Place At Playhead button. (Of course, Place At Playhead is a bit more precise.) Once you have the audio on one of the audio tracks (the lowest track is usually best), it's ready for you to edit its length, volume, or fade-in and fade-out characteristics.

10

Chapter 11

Troubleshoot iTunes

How to…

- Troubleshoot iTunes
- Solve Problems with Songs
- Deal with File Corruption
- Fix Burning Issues
- Create a Backup Plan
- Get More Help

Hopefully, you won't have too much trouble with iTunes. It's a well-written application based on fairly rock-solid technology—particularly QuickTime, which has been around for years now, and is continually improving. Of course, all that happy talk is probably downright annoying if you've come to this chapter because of something frustrating, like iTunes *won't recognize your darned CD!*

I'd like to take a look at some of the known issues, such as those that Apple officially recognizes, as well as some general troubleshooting advice culled from my experience and from online discussions. Then, I'd like to encourage you to back up your music library and other key items so you can restore iTunes if you ever have trouble and/or if you decide to move to a new computer at some point.

Troubleshoot iTunes

Problems you'll encounter with iTunes tend to be of two types. The first is playback problems—the file doesn't sound good or there are gaps, hisses, or pops in playback. Sometimes this is due to corruption in the files that iTunes uses for daily operations—a music file, the iTunes database, and so on—and other times, it may have to do with a setting, preferences, or some problem you're having with your computer hardware.

The second is trouble with an external device and, in particular, CD and CD-RW drives. If you can't get a drive to mount a CD or you can't seem to burn a disc correctly and so on, then you're probably in good company—that's the sort of problem that crops up a lot with a program like iTunes.

You'll also find that some issues simply appear more often with the Mac version than the Windows version (or vice versa). And you'll find, in this chapter, that I know a lot more about the problems with the Mac version because it's been around for a few years now and the Windows version has been out only a short time as of this writing.

So I'll try to cover both, but please visit www.mac-upgrade.com/itunes for more updates on both Mac and Windows troubleshooting issues as they come to light.

NOTE   *If you're having trouble launching iTunes, it may be because another user on your Mac or PC already has it running. Both Mac OS X and Windows XP are capable of fast user switching, allowing multiple users to be logged into the computer. Each has a "suspend" mode that enables you to switch between user accounts. However, in both cases if iTunes is running in one user account, it can't be launched in another user account, even if that first user account is inactive. You'll need to switch to the account where iTunes is open, close it, and then switch back to your account to launch it again.*

Sound and Skipping Problems

If you have trouble with the volume or playback of your songs, the first place to look for the culprit is in the iTunes Preferences. Open the Preferences dialog box and choose the Effects icon or tab. Both Sound Enhancer and Sound Check are designed to automatically change the sound levels as well as certain qualities of the native digital music files. Experiment with turning those settings on and off to see if they change the sound quality at all.

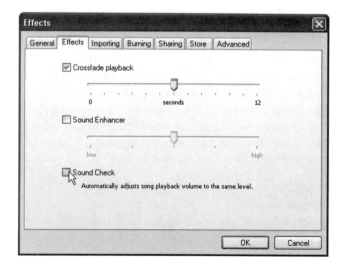

If your songs seem to be playing with a different level of sound quality than they have in the past, you might want to check the equalizer (EQ) settings. Click the EQ button in the bottom-right corner of the iTunes window or choose Window |

EQ (in the Mac version). When the EQ window appears, check the settings to see if they've changed or if they're set to something that doesn't make sense for your current configuration. (For instance, the settings Bass Reducer or Vocal Booster may do odd things you're not expecting.) As a test, you can try simply turning the EQ off to see if it makes a significant difference:

If your songs skip during playback, this could be due to one of several reasons, including:

- **Song location** Songs located in different parts of your hard disk or on external disks may exhibit problems (or to put it another way, they may exhibit problems different from those files stored in your main iTunes folder). For starters, you can try using the Advanced | Consolidate Library command to copy all your songs to the same place.

- **Bothersome network traffic** Pauses may be par for the course if you're listening to streaming MP3s or Internet "radio" stations since sometimes network traffic can get in the way of a perfect stream. You should make sure you're using a stream that will download comfortably over your Internet connection. A modem-based connection can't handle anything over 56 kbps, for instance, and often can't handle a connection that wide—24 or 32 kbps may be a better choice.

- **A hard-working system** If your Mac is already working hard on other tasks, you may encounter skipping and pausing in iTunes. Try quitting other applications that are running in the background or wait for very intensive tasks (such as burning data CDs or rendering complex graphics) to complete before attempting to use iTunes.

- **Disk fragmentation** After a while, disk fragmentation can cause playback trouble. After months or years of use, your hard drive will have portions of files scattered all over it as files are deleted and written and deleted again.

The less contiguous these files are, the slower their retrieval can be, particularly if the disk has become severely fragmented. On the Mac, you can use a third-party utility designed for your version of the Mac OS to combat fragmentation. In Windows, you can use the built-in Disk Defragmenter, which is found at Start | Accessories | System Tools | Disk Defragmenter (see Figure 11-1).

■ **Ongoing background tasks**   Running certain background tasks, like file sharing, running an Internet server, or doing low-level work such as disk defragmenting or automated backups, can cause slowdowns that you're not aware of but that cause iTunes trouble. On the Mac, certain users have gotten better results from iTunes by disabling directory services they don't need because they're not on a complex network. In the Utilities folder, find and launch Directory Access and then turn off any services you don't need to use. (For a home user, the only necessary services are likely to be AppleTalk and Rendezvous unless you have a cross-platform network, in which case SMB may be important. You should consult a book about the Mac OS to be certain of your choices, however.)

Volume	Session Status	File System	Capacity	Free Space	% Free Space
HP_RECOVERY (D:)		FAT32	5.55 GB	992 MB	17 %
HP_PAVILION (C:)	Analyzed	NTFS	31.70 GB	24.61 GB	77 %

FIGURE 11-1   Disk Defragmenter in Windows is an important tool to use every few months.

Corruption Problems

With any computer program, corruption is a potential problem. With iTunes, there's a good chance you'll encounter some corruption at some point because iTunes is constantly working with multiple files and writing data to a number of others, such as the iTunes music database and the iTunes preferences file. Every time iTunes opens a file to write to it, there's at least a chance that the file could become corrupted, particularly if iTunes crashes or if you encounter other system-level programs.

The solution in most of these cases is to simply allow iTunes to rebuild its various databases. On a Mac, that's a two-parter. In Windows, the best plan is to restore your library, as discussed later in the section "Back Up and Restore."

The Mac version of iTunes relies heavily on its preference file, which is stored in your home folder, inside the Library folder, in a subfolder called Preferences. The file is called com.apple.iTunes.plist. The types of problems the preferences file is likely to cause include an inability to launch iTunes, problems once it's running (including crashes that appear to happen "for no reason"), and trouble that you have with settings in iTunes Preferences or when changing those settings. To troubleshoot the preferences file, quit iTunes and move the preferences file from the Preferences folder to a folder outside of the Library hierarchy—to your desktop or Documents folder, for instance. Now, restart iTunes and test to see if that fixes the problem. If it doesn't, you can return the preferences file to your Preferences folder, overwriting the new one that was created. (Or, you can continue to work with the new one without worry—you may need to reset some preferences, but that's about it.) If it does fix the problem, you can delete the old preferences file and, in iTunes, reset any preferences lost in the transaction.

NOTE   *The truth is, many Mac troubleshooters will delete the preferences file of a problematic application with little provocation, because doing so doesn't really harm anything. (You may have to reset some preferences within iTunes after the preference file has been deleted and the program launched again, but that's the only major drawback.)*

Deleting the preferences file in iTunes for Mac does something else important—it causes iTunes to revert to its "first-time launched" state. This brings up the iTunes Assistant, which asks if you'd like to search your hard disk for music files. So, coupled with deleting the iTunes Music File, the following is a fairly common remedy if you're having trouble with your iTunes Library:

1. Shut down iTunes.

2. Delete the iTunes Music Library file that's in your main iTunes folder (probably in your Music folder, but you may have chosen to put it elsewhere).

3. Delete the iTunes preferences file.

4. Restart iTunes and allow the iTunes Assistant to search your drive for music files.

After searching, you'll see the iTunes window appear and you'll have a full library of songs, if they were found on your hard disk. What you won't have is a full set of playlists in the source list—you'll need to either re-create them or restore them from backups that you've made in the past (see the section "Back Up and Restore") later in this chapter.

One final Mac-specific corruption problem: sometimes permissions in Mac OS X can become corrupted, causing all sorts of odd problems and slowdowns in Mac OS X. The solution is to fix those permissions using a special Apple tool. Launch Disk Utility (found in the Utilities folder inside your Mac's main Applications folder) and select the relevant disk (the one with iTunes on it or the one with the problematic songs) in the window. Now, make sure the First Aid tab is selected and click the Repair Disk Permissions button (see Figure 11-2). You'll see the Disk Utility get started, looking for and fixing problems with permissions. (You can also use the Repair Disk command to look for other solutions—in Mac OS X, it seems that Repair Permissions will sometimes cause applications to spring to life when Repair Disk doesn't.)

Songs that Won't Play

Most often, the reason a song won't play is because of rights protection. If you're trying to play a protected AAC song (that was bought from the iTunes Music Store) under certain circumstances, it won't work. For instance, you can't play a protected AAC song in a copy of iTunes that isn't authorized for that song—when you try, you'll see a dialog box asking you to enter the Apple ID and password associated with that song. Likewise, you can't play a protected AAC song using the Shared Music feature in iTunes if your computer isn't authorized for the song, even if the computer that's doing the sharing *is*—iTunes will just skip protected songs. The solution is to authorize the remote computer as well, if you're able to. (See Chapter 4 for details on song authorization.)

Apple notes in its Knowledge Base that not all AAC files are compatible with iTunes. iTunes can play back MPEG-4 AAC songs, but not other types. (But those AAC files can still show up in the iTunes window.) So, if you run across another

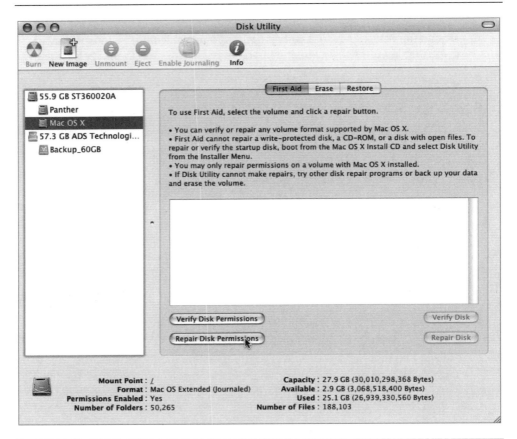

FIGURE 11-2   Use the Repair Disk Permissions command on the First Aid tab of Disk Utility for troubleshooting general slowdowns or odd crashing.

type of song and attempt to play it in iTunes, you'll encounter an error or a failure. Note that other types of digital audio files, such as Real Media and Windows Media audio files, are also incompatible with iTunes.

Problems with Song Titles and Information

Sometimes a song that's imported into iTunes will end up with an odd-looking title; in particular, if the MP3 was originally encoded in a different application, there may be a problem with the ID3 tag for that MP3. An ID3 tag is a small bit of data that's embedded in an MP3 file and includes information about the album, artist, and so on. (It's actually an informal standard, not a part of the MP3 official standard, but it's widely recognized by MP3 players.) AAC files use a different system, and various types of ID3 tag versions have been used over time.

When you edit the name or album information of an MP3 stored in your iTunes Library, you're altering its ID3 tag, so if you were to load that file on another computer, it should have its information intact. It's also true that you can lose some of this information when you convert MP3 files to AAC files.

If you have trouble with a particular song's title or similar information, select it in the iTunes Library and choose Advanced | Convert ID3 Tags. You can then choose to either change the type of ID3 tag (turn on the option ID3 Tag Version and choose a version from the menu) or turn on Translate Text Characters, which enables you to experiment with different encoding schemes that may have been used for the MP3's name. Click OK to see if the conversion improves the look of the song's information.

If converting the ID3 tag doesn't work, you can edit the name, artist, and so on directly within the library by clicking an entry, waiting a second and then clicking the word (title, artist, album) again. Or, you can edit all the information for a song by selecting it, choosing File | Get Info, and then clicking the Info tab. Make your edits and click OK.

Want to try a more automated approach? If your Internet connection is active, select a song and choose Advanced | Get CD Track Names to look up the track in the CDDB. It won't always work with imported songs, but it's worth a try.

Shareware tools like ID3X for Mac (www.three-2-one.de/321apps) or Zortam ID3 Tag Editor for Windows (www.zortam.com/product-id3te.html) are handy ways to dig deeper into ID3 settings.

Trouble with CDs

If you're having trouble using a consumer or car stereo to play back a CD you burned in iTunes, you should check for two things. First, most car stereos and many consumer stereos can't play back MP3 CDs (although many new models can). You'll have to look for a device that's compatible with the MP3 CD or go back and burn the songs you want to hear to an audio CD. Also, you should check the media you used during the burning process since many consumer devices have trouble playing back any type of CD that was burned to CD-RW media; CD-R media is much more reliable in car and home stereos.

11

TIP   *There are plenty of new consumer CD players and stereo components (as well as DVD players) that are compatible with MP3 CDs. In most cases, they play back the songs just as if you were listening to an audio CD. The only difference is you'll have many more "tracks" at your disposal, since many more compressed MP3 songs fit on an MP3 CD. Some more advanced components will include song and artist information using data from the MP3 files.*

If you're having trouble importing songs from CDs, this may be due to several possible reasons. First, it's possible that you have a CD that's copy protected—they're becoming more common. The first way to troubleshoot a CD that doesn't allow you to import songs is to try importing from another CD—that tells you that your CD player and iTunes are working well together. If you can import from other CD players, chances are the CD is the problem—check its materials or contact the disc's publisher to see if it's copy protected.

NOTE   *One sign that a disc is copy protected is that it won't play back in your computer's CD drive (as opposed to a consumer CD player). Some manufacturers introduce slight errors into the disc to make them less compatible with computers—the idea being that it will thwart digital copies.*

If you encounter songs that "drop out" or portions of the playback seem to be missing, you should open iTunes Preferences, click the Importing icon and ensure that the option Use Error Correction When Reading Audio CDs is turned on.

If you have trouble burning songs to CDs using iTunes, the first two items to consider are whether your CD-RW (or DVD-RW) drive is compatible with iTunes and whether you're using good CD-R media. The compatibility issue is generally only a problem with external CD-RW drives on the Mac since Apple provides the internal drives on iTunes-compatible Macs. Of course, compatibility can be a problem for nearly any Windows user because Apple has less of an idea of the mechanism you have installed in the PC.

Most recent third-party and PC-based CD/DVD burning drives work fine with iTunes. If you're having trouble with such a drive on a Mac, you should open iTunes Preferences and click the Burning icon. If the drive is listed, then it's recognized and it should work OK. If it's not listed, consult the manufacturer's web site and check Apple's storage compatibility web site (www.apple.com/macosx/upgrade/storage.html).

If you have trouble with a PC device, you can also consult the Burning screen in iTunes Preferences. If your drive is listed in the dialog box, it should work.

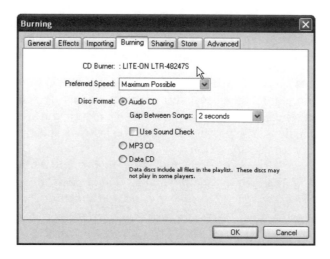

If it's not listed, you may have a driver issue. Consult your PC and/or CD/DVD burner manufacturer and see if they have updated driver software or a firmware update for that drive. You should also make sure you have recently used the Windows Update feature so that the latest versions of any Windows fixes are present on your computer.

In the meantime, here are some general troubleshooting tips for both platforms when it comes to burning CDs:

- Make sure your computer is not set to go to sleep at all while a burn is happening. You can have the monitor or display shut down after a while, but make sure both the hard disk and the processor are set to stay awake for the burn. (On the Mac, that's the Energy Saver pane in System Preferences; in Windows, you choose Power Options in the Control Panel.)

- Some users report that they have better luck when setting the gap between songs (on the Burning screen in iTunes Preferences) to something less than five seconds. Say, two or three seconds.

- If iTunes can't seem to get successfully through the burn process—or if the final CD isn't usable—try choosing a lower speed in the Preferred Speed menu on the Burning screen in iTunes Preferences. This is particularly true if your drive is a few years old. Some users report having luck burning as slow as 2x when they've had trouble at faster speeds.

11

■ Try different brands of CD-R media, particularly if the burn process seems to go OK, but the discs won't play back (or will only play back on certain drives). Some brands simply work better with some drives and, of course, some brands offer a higher quality level than others. For discs that you intend to keep a while (such as audio CDs you create), you might want to invest in a premium brand of CD-R media.

■ Apple notes specifically that if you use CD-RW media for audio CDs (which isn't a great idea because, as I mentioned earlier, consumer equipment tends to work better with CD-R media), you should use CD-RW media that's specifically made for 1x to 4x speeds.

NOTE   *Having trouble burning songs that you bought from the iTunes Music Store? Usually it works well, but there's one circumstance where iTunes may simply up and stop burning your bought songs: if you've burned ten CDs from the same playlist. The solution? Just move the songs around on the playlist. iTunes will let you burn your bought songs all you want, but it doesn't want you knocking off copy after copy without a little inconvenience.*

Finally, one last bit of advice if you have trouble getting iTunes to successfully complete a burn—quit all open applications. In our modern OSes, Mac OS X, and Windows 2000/XP, that can sometimes be easier said than done because of all the background processes that go on. Try turning off network services, e-mail applications, automatic alerts, and anything else that might be popping up and interfering with the burn process.

NOTE   *These sorts of technical problems are always a moving target, so it's not helpful to focus too much on specific problems and error messages in this section. See the section "Find Answers" later in this chapter for pointers on where to go for current support and help resources on the Internet. Indeed, the Web is the best place to find the latest chatter about a problem you might be experiencing.*

Fix Trouble Downloading Music Files

Because the iTunes Music Store requires that you access Internet services and jump through a few hoops to complete a transaction, there are errors. Apple documents some of the error messages you can encounter in its Knowledge Base in article

#93431 (http://docs.info.apple.com/article.html?artnum=93431). Let's quickly go over these now:

- -9800, -9815, or -9814 errors (or downloaded songs won't play) on a Mac often mean that the clock (date) on your Mac isn't set correctly. Open System Preferences and choose the Date & Time panel. Set the clock and date and try again.

- An "Unable to Complete Your Request" error when you're trying to create an Apple account or access your Apple account information in Windows that doesn't seem to be related to a bad Internet connection may also be because you don't have the date and time set correctly. Open the Control Panel and set the date and time (the choice is "Date, Time, Language, and Regional Options").

- "Unable to check," -5000, -35 or "Unable to contact store" errors in the Mac version could mean that there's a problem with your Internet connection to the store. If that doesn't appear to be the case (if your Internet connection seems to be working otherwise), then it's possible that permissions are set incorrectly for the iTunes Music folder that you've selected, or that folder may be missing. Check that the folder exists and that you're set to use it on the Advanced screen of iTunes Preferences. If all that looks right, you may need to correct the permissions on that folder. Consult article #93069 in the Knowledge Base (http://docs.info.apple.com/article.html?artnum=93069) for instructions on fixing the permissions.

- According to Apple, error -39 or trouble accessing parts of the iTunes Music store in the Windows version may result from using special web acceleration or filtering software is installed such as the Earthlink Accelerator. Turn the accelerator off for best results; with a filter, it should be set to allow you to access the servers phobos.apple.com and phobos.apple.com.edgesuite .net, according to article #93434 in the Knowledge Base (http://docs.info.apple .com/article.html?artnum=93434).

If you have trouble with iTunes when it's in the middle of a download, you should be able to resume that download the next time you launch iTunes and connect to the Internet. Simply select Advanced | Check for Purchased Music and iTunes will check for songs that weren't completely downloaded previously.

11

Update iTunes

In some cases, the only real solution to a problem with iTunes is for Apple to release an official update to the software. In my experience, Apple is pretty good at releasing frequent updates to software, particularly when those updates can fix problems and get the software working for more people. (And this has been even truer ever since the Internet came into wider use because it makes these sorts of updates so easy to distribute.) But the question is: how do you get these updates?

You can take a few different approaches. Any user—Mac or Windows—can head to www.apple.com/support/itunes to check on tips and tricks and to see if a new version of iTunes has been posted for your operating system. (To know what version you currently have, choose iTunes | About iTunes in the Mac version and Help | About iTunes in Windows.)

In Mac OS X, iTunes is included in the group of applications that Apple will automatically update (or alert you to updates) using the Software Update features. If you'd like to check immediately for updates, open the System Preferences application and click the Software Update icon to open its pane (see Figure 11-3). Click the Check Now button to have the Mac OS check for updates. You can also use the pane to check for updates automatically.

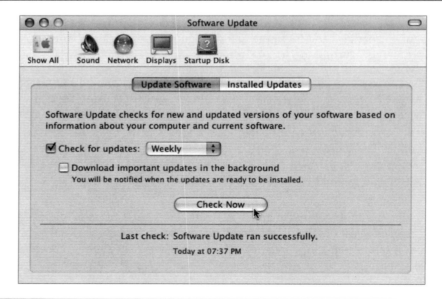

FIGURE 11-3 The Software Update pane can be used to update many of your Apple-written Mac applications, including iTunes.

In Windows, you can't automate the process, but you *can* check for updates to iTunes easily. Choose Help | Check For Updates and iTunes will check Apple's servers for updates to iTunes for Windows.

If one is found, you'll be able to download and install it to (hopefully) improve your copy of iTunes.

Back Up and Restore

Problems with your hard disk can happen. In fact, every hard disk ever made is guaranteed to go bad at some point (it may take years or even decades, but it'll happen). Hard disks have a lot of moving parts and they're destined to fail over time, which is why a backup copy of any computer data is important. With iTunes, particularly if you buy music from the iTunes Music Store, backing up can save you time and money. First, with bought songs, there's no other recourse to recovering those songs if you don't do backups and then later lose your library to a disk problem or some other catastrophe. Even if you have your receipts, Apple will insist you pay again for any songs you want that previously downloaded. With songs you've imported from CDs, you can recover a lost library by reimporting your songs, but it's much easier if you back up your music as data files, so you don't have to go through the track importing process for every CD-based song in your library.

Fortunately, backing up is fairly simple. The best plan is to use iTunes' built-in ability to burn data CDs to your advantage—you can use iTunes to back up your files to CD (or DVD), which you can then use for recovery later, if necessary. You can also use a hard disk for backup—for instance, if you have an extra external drive—and that's certainly a handy solution since it simply requires you to copy your iTunes Music folder from your main hard disk to that external disk. Unless you store the disk well away from your computer, however, that sort of backup is of limited use. After all, if a catastrophe (such as a fire or storm) strikes your computer, chances are it will destroy the external hard disk sitting next to it, too. So, a CD or DVD can be a handy way to not only back up your music, but also store that backup in a different place—a safety deposit box or some other secondary location is always a great idea.

To back up to a CD or DVD, first copy your entire library to a playlist. (You can call it "Backup" or something similar.) Now, simply walk through the steps

11

to create a data CD as described in Chapter 3. The cool part, as you may know, is that iTunes will actually split your library over multiple CDs or DVDs, if multiples are required, automatically prompting you for the next CD.

 *Using a playlist and iTunes for your backup is quite convenient since every song gets copied to the data CD (if it's available to iTunes) even if it's not currently stored in your iTunes Music folder. That's one advantage over third-party backup software, for instance. If you store all of your music in the iTunes Music folder by default, however, this shouldn't be a pressing issue.*

Now, once you have a CD of your iTunes library, you may find yourself in a situation where you don't necessarily want to re-burn the entire library every few weeks or months, even though you've added songs to the library by purchasing them or importing them from CDs. Fortunately, you don't have to. Instead, you can use iTunes' smart playlist technology to create a playlist that automatically includes all of the songs since your last backup. All you need to know is the date when you last backed them up. Here's how to create the playlist:

1. Choose File | New Smart Playlist.

2. In the Smart Playlist window, choose Date Added from the first menu. Then select Is After from the second menu and enter the date of your most recent backup in the entry box.

3. Make sure Live Updating is selected and click OK.

The result will be an untitled playlist in the source list that you can name. Then, check the playlist and you should see all of the songs that you've imported or purchased since the date you used for the smart playlist. Now, with the playlist selected, click Burn Disc and walk through the process to back up all of these additional songs.

When you add new songs in the future, you can back them up simply by selecting the playlist you created, choosing File | Edit Smart Playlist and changing the date since the most recent backup.

Find Answers

As mentioned, this chapter can't be terribly specific because new versions of iTunes come out all the time to address specific problems in older versions (while, at the same time, sometimes introducing new problems of their own). So, to stay on top of the exact troubleshooting needs of your particular version of iTunes, the best place to look is the Web.

Apple's support site offers a few different places you should look into, and there are other sites on the Internet as well that offer information. Here's a quick list:

- **The Apple iTunes page (www.apple.com/itunes)**   While the main iTunes page is mostly sales and marketing copy, it will sometimes link to new versions of the software and when something is downloadable, it's generally available from this page.

- **The Apple iTunes for Mac Support page (www.apple.com/support/itunes)**   On this page, you'll find support Q&A information, support articles, tips, and the ability to search the Knowledge Base.

- **The Apple iTunes for Windows Support page (www.info.apple.com/usen/itunes/windows)**   This offers the same sort of options: Q&A, support search, and downloads for Windows.

- **Apple Support Discussions (http://discussions.info.apple.com)**   In these pages, you'll find forums that enable you to ask questions and get answers from other iTunes users. Apple doesn't have much of an official presence on these boards, but you'll find lots of power users and people who hang out on the boards trying to help others.

- **iPodLounge (www.ipodlounge.com/forums)**   This is a third-party site run by Dennis Lloyd that offers lots of news regarding the iPod and iTunes, as well as discussion forums, links to support, classifieds, and quite a bit more.

- **HTDE with iTunes (www.mac-upgrade.com/itunes)**   The official page for this book, with links to important sites, Q&As, discussions, and so on.

Appendix A

Get and Install iTunes

How to...

- Get and Install iTunes for Mac
- Get and Install iTunes for Windows

Get and Install iTunes for Mac

If you don't have a copy of iTunes and your Mac is compatible with it, you can get it on CD-ROM as part of the iLife bundle of applications that Apple sells in retail stores and at www.apple.com/store/ on the Internet. (It is not necessary to buy iLife, however, since iTunes is available as a free download.) For iTunes 4, you'll need a Mac that's running Mac OS X 10.1.5 or later (Mac OS X 10.2.4 or later is required if you want to share music over a network or burn DVD-R discs using iTunes) and at least a 400 MHz PowerPC G3 or G4 processor. Apple also recommends at least 256MB of RAM.

If you have an older version of iTunes or the Mac OS and you don't want to buy the retail package, you should be able to download the latest version from www.itunes.com as Apple, at least as of this writing, is giving iTunes away to any interested party. (Of course, giving it away is a good idea for Apple, since the real revenue stream is the iTunes Store discussed in Chapter 4.)

On the main iTunes page, you'll find a link that you can click in order to download the latest version. You'll then most likely be asked to enter a name and e-mail address—do so and click the Download iTunes button. Now, sit back and wait while the download comes to you. When it's done, you'll have the application's installer downloaded as a *disk image*, which is a file that can be mounted on your desktop as if it were an external disk. It should actually be mounted automatically after it downloads—if not, locate and double-click the file, which is probably called something like `iTunes4.x.dmg`. Once the disk image is mounted, you can access it as if it were a CD or similar external disks. Open it up in the Finder and you'll see a Legal Agreement screen; read the agreement and then click Agree. A window will appear and you'll see the iTunes package file.

 *If you use Apple's Safari browser for the download, then you may have a folder on your desktop (or in your download folder, if it's different from the desktop) called iTunes. Open that folder to launch the installer.*

iTunes4.mpkg

Double-click that file and you'll launch the installer application. You can now walk through the onscreen steps in order to get iTunes installed:

1. Read the Welcome screen. If a dialog sheet appears asking you if an application can be run, click Continue in the dialog sheet. Then, click Continue again on the Welcome screen.

2. On the Important Information screen, you can read any last minute items that Apple thinks you should know about this version of iTunes. That might include problems, incompatibilities, or recommendations that are worth taking a look at. When you're done, click Continue.

3. Now on the Select A Destination screen, choose the disk where you would like to install iTunes. This is something of an academic choice, as you can only install iTunes on the same disk from which you've started up your Mac. (As you'll see in Chapter 2, you can store your music files in other places once you've installed and configured iTunes.) Select your local hard disk and click Continue.

4. Now you're set for an Easy Install, which is your only choice. (You can click Customize if you're curious to see what happens, but you aren't actually given a choice as to what gets installed.) Click Install to begin the installation process.

5. At this point, you may be asked to authenticate by signing in with your Mac OS X name and password. Enter these, and then click OK.

6. If the Installer accepts your name and password, the application will be installed. When it's done, you'll see the message, "The software was successfully installed." Click Close to close the installer application. iTunes is now installed.

Uninstall iTunes

In Mac OS X, there isn't much reason to uninstall iTunes—if you opt not to use it, it shouldn't cause any trouble if you simply leave it in the Applications folder unattended. If, for some reason, you simply don't want it on your computer, you can uninstall the program very easily—simply drag the iTunes icon from the Applications folder to the Trash. (You may need to enter an Administrator's name and password to accomplish this if you aren't already logged into an admin account.) Deleting the iTunes application doesn't delete your music files, nor does it delete your iTunes Music Library files or your iTunes preferences, so you can reinstall and launch iTunes at any time if you'd like to access your music again.

A

 *Before uninstalling iTunes, you may want to launch it and choose Advanced | Deauthorize Computer, which causes this computer to no longer be authorized for playing back music you've bought via iTunes Music Store. That frees up one of the three computers you're allowed to authorize to play back such music. (If you've never bought music from the iTunes Music Store, this shouldn't be an issue.)*

Updating iTunes

iTunes can be automatically updated using the Software Update feature in Mac OS X. If you've got an Internet connection, this is the easiest way to get the latest version of iTunes from Apple. To launch Software Update, choose it from the Apple menu in Mac OS X 10.3 or later. In earlier Mac OS X versions, you first launch the System Preferences application (choose Apple menu | System Preferences) and then click the Software Update icon in System Preferences.

When you launch Software Update directly on Mac OS X 10.3 and later, it will immediately attempt to connect to Apple's Software Update servers over the Internet. If the connection is successful, the Software Update screen will appear (shown in Figure A-1), and you'll be able to choose the updates you'd like to download and install.

If you access the Software Update pane in the System Preferences application, you can get to the screen shown in Figure A-1 by clicking the Check Now button on the Update Software tab, as shown here.

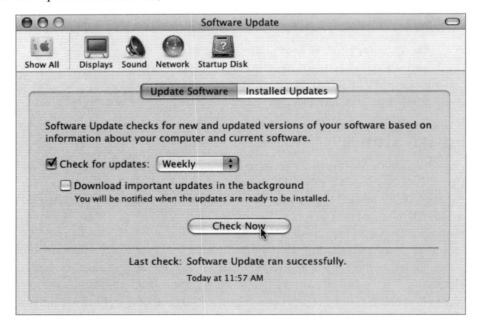

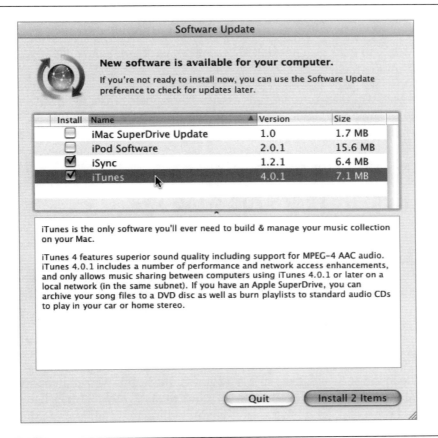

FIGURE A-1   The Software Update screen enables you to select the updates you want to install.

A

You can also use the Software Update pane in System Preferences to schedule automatic checking of Apple's servers for updates.

Here's how Software Update works:

1. Once the Software Update window is up, you can place a check mark next to the items you'd like to download and install. (You can also click the name of each update to get an explanation of that update, as shown in Figure A-1.) Click the Install button (it may say "Install *x* Items") to begin the download and installation process.

2. After you click Install, you may be asked to authenticate by signing in with your Mac OS X username and password. Do so, and then click OK.

3. Now you may see an installation agreement. Read it and click Agree if you want to proceed.

Your Mac will then automatically retrieve the updates from the Apple servers and install them, updating you as the process continues. When the update is done, you'll be returned to the Software Update window if you have other un-downloaded updates. You can click Quit if you're finished, and then begin computing immediately since iTunes doesn't require a restart of your Mac.

Get and Install iTunes for Windows

iTunes for Windows has relatively stiff requirements, the most important being that you must be running Windows 2000 or Windows XP (earlier versions are not compatible). Apple's requirements include a 500 MHz or better Pentium-class processor, at least 128MB of RAM (256MB recommended) and QuickTime 6.4, which is included and installed along with iTunes. It's also recommended that you have a CD-RW or DVD-R drive that's supported by iTunes, and a high-speed Internet connection.

Get iTunes for Windows

To download the software, head to www.itunes.com on the Web and choose to download the Windows version. After you click the Download iTunes button, you should see a dialog box that asks if you're willing to install and run the file that Apple is sending you.

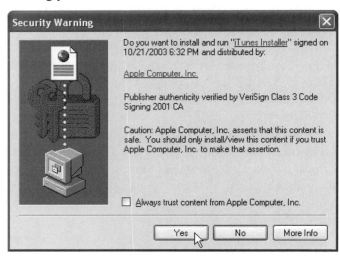

In most cases, the Installer Wizard will launch automatically. If it doesn't, you may see a dialog box asking if you'd like to open or save the file that you're downloading. If you'd like the installer to launch immediately after download, choose Open; otherwise, you can choose Save if you'd like to run the installer on your own terms. If you choose save, you'll see a Save As dialog box that enables you to choose a location for the file.

Install iTunes for Windows

Once the installer is downloaded, either it will launch automatically or you can double-click, the file iTunesSetup to launch the InstallShield Wizard, which will walk you through the installation process. Here's how the wizard works:

1. The first screen is a welcome screen—read the text and click Next.

2. The second screen is the License Agreement. Read through the agreement (there's a scroll bar on the right side of the window) and then click the Yes button to accept the agreement and move to the next screen.

3. The third screen is the Information screen. Here you'll read about late changes to the software or, in some cases, known problems. Click Next after you've read the document.

4. On the Setup Type screen, you can place check marks next to the options you want enabled. You can choose whether you want desktop icons for iTunes and QuickTime (turning this option off means their icons will only be placed in the Start menu) and whether iTunes and/or QuickTime should be used as the default players for media files. With these options turned on, iTunes will be used for Internet audio playback, streaming MP3s, and other sound files; QuickTime will be used for QuickTime movies, AVI movies, and a lot of streaming content, but not for Windows Media or RealPlayer content, which QuickTime can't play back. Click Next to continue.

5. On the Choose Destination Location screen, click the Browse button if you'd like to have iTunes installed to a directory other than the one shown (C:\Program Files\iTunes). Click Next to continue.

6. On the next screen, the installer is simply telling you it's ready to begin. (It actually shows you an ad-like image of happy people with iPods, at least as of this writing.) Click Next to begin the installation process. You'll move to a screen that shows you the progress of the installation.

A

7. On the Installation Successful screen, the installer asks if you want to restart your computer. Click the radio button next to Yes and click Finish to begin the restart process, or click No and Finish if you'd like to restart later. (Your PC must reboot for QuickTime to start.)

Start Up iTunes for Windows

Once your PC restarts after the installation process is finished, you should be ready to use iTunes. Locate its icon on the desktop or choose it from the Start menu—by default, you'll find it by choosing Start | All Programs | iTunes | iTunes. Also, before you start up iTunes, remember that it's a good idea to have your Internet connection up and running if you have the type of Internet connection that requires you to initiate a connection (such as some modem dial-up, ISDN connections, and DSL connections).

When you launch iTunes for the first time, you'll see the iTunes Setup Assistant, which walks you through some final steps:

1. On the Welcome screen, click Next once you've read the welcome text.

2. On the Find Music Screen, you'll make the decision as to whether or not iTunes should look in your My Music folder for music files. Choose Yes if you want it to and No if you don't want it to look through your My Music folder and automatically add any music it finds to iTunes. Then click Next.

3. On the Keep iTunes Music Folder Organized screen, click Yes if you don't mind letting iTunes rearrange the files and folders of the music that it finds in your My Music folder; click No if you want it to keep the folders the way it found them. Click Next to continue.

4. On the iTunes Music Store screen, click Yes if you want iTunes to open up and immediately go to the Music Store or click No if you want to open up to the regular iTunes Library. Note that this is a one-time thing—by default, iTunes will always open up to the iTunes Library. Click Finish.

That's it. iTunes should launch and you'll now be ready to work with it given the instructions in Chapter 1. Congratulations!

Uninstall iTunes for Windows

Want to uninstall iTunes for Windows? Locate the iTunesSetup file and double-click it. You'll get an option to uninstall iTunes. If you can't find the iTunesSetup file, then choose Start | Control Panel. In the Control Panel, select Add or Remove

Programs. A list of programs that can be uninstalled will appear. Choose iTunes and click the Change/Remove button. You'll see the InstallShield Wizard again. On the Welcome screen, choose Remove and click Next. Confirm that you want to remove the files in the Confirm Uninstall dialog box and Windows will begin the uninstall process.

Note that even though iTunes will be completely uninstalled, your music files and even your iTunes preferences files will remain untouched. This way, if you install iTunes again, you'll pick up pretty much where you left off. Also, you must use Add or Remove Programs separately if you want to uninstall QuickTime.

NOTE   *Before uninstalling iTunes for Windows, you may want to launch it and choose Advanced | Deauthorize Computer, which causes your current computer to no longer be authorized to play back music you've bought via iTunes Music Store. Apple only allows three computers to be authorized at any one time, so deauthorizing the system you're currently using means you could authorize another one later. (If you've never bought music from the iTunes Music Store, this shouldn't be an issue.)*

A

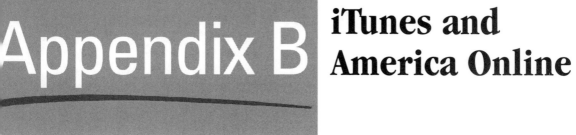

Appendix B

iTunes and America Online

How to...

■ Use iTunes with Your AOL Account

■ Use AOL to Access the iTunes Store

AOL and iTunes

Apple and America Online (AOL) work together to make the iTunes Music Store accessible to AOL users on two different levels. From within iTunes, you can sign into the iTunes Music Store using your AOL account name and password—songs and albums you buy will actually be billed to your AOL account unless you opt to pay by the shopping cart method. And you don't have to be signed into AOL to use that account—you can use your AOL account name and password even if you're directly connected to the iTunes Music Store over the Internet.

Use Your AOL Account with iTunes

Regardless of how you connect or pay, your AOL account automatically gains you access to the iTunes Store and can be used for storing preferences and to set up iTunes to playback iTunes Music Store songs.

Here's how to use your AOL account to sign into the iTunes Music Store:

1. Launch the store from within iTunes by choosing Music Store from the Source list.

2. To sign in, click the Account box where it likely says Sign In. (If you see an account name there, you'll need to click it, then click Sign Out on the dialog box that appears.)

3. In the unlabeled dialog box, click the radio button next to AOL and enter your AOL screen name and password.

4. If iTunes Music Store is able to verify your account name and password, you'll see a dialog box that tells you that the account hasn't yet been used with iTunes Music Store, and you'll be asked to review your account information. Click the Review button.

5. Now you'll likely see some legalese. Read up and click the Agree button if you agree with the terms of the license and the way in which Apple and AOL will be taking your money.

6. Next, you'll choose the billing arrangement from those that you have stored in your AOL Wallet (or you can enter different info by selecting Enter New Billing Information). Click Next.

7. Depending on the state of your billing, you may see another screen that asks you to confirm or add a different card. Otherwise, you should see a congratulatory screen where you're able to click Done.

With your account established, you can buy songs just as discussed in Chapter 4.

As part of its deal with AOL, the iTunes Music Store offers Sessions@AOL recordings for sale—these are special recordings by popular artists that are unique to AOL, but that are now also offered through iTunes.

B

Use AOL to Access the iTunes Music Store

When you are connected to AOL, you have two ways to access music in the iTunes Music Store. First, you can actually run iTunes—it should be able to use your AOL connection as an Internet connection in order to allow you access to the iTunes Music Store. Second, you can also buy songs via the iTunes Music Store from within AOL.

> **NOTE** *As of this writing, most of the AOL internal features discussed here seem only to work in the Windows version of AOL, including Radio@AOL and most of the audio playback features.*

In the AOL Music section (keyword: Music), for instance, you'll find links from songs in the Listening Lounge archive and elsewhere that enable you to listen to full cuts of popular songs (usually at lower quality and with the occasional AOL tagline to discourage you from simply copying the song). In those situations, you'll see a link to iTunes, which should automatically launch iTunes and show you the song you're listening to so that you can buy it in iTunes.

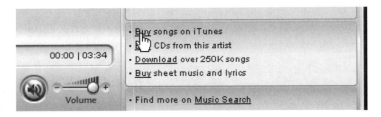

Another place where the iTunes link appears is in Radio@AOL, where some songs, if they're available in the iTunes Music Store database, show up with a Buy Song link in their window. Click the link and you're taken to iTunes so that you can access the song in the iTunes Music Store.

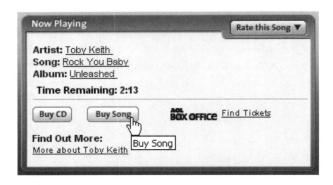

Appendix C iTunes and iLife '04

How to...

- Use iTunes with iMovie
- Use iTunes with iDVD
- Use iTunes with iPhoto
- Use iTunes with GarageBand

iTunes for the Macintosh isn't just a standalone application. It's really part of a suite of applications, called iLife, that Apple provides with new Macs and makes available for retail purchase for older Macs. The key to this suite of applications is that they can work together to extend their capabilities. In this appendix, I'd like to quickly explore the ways that iTunes can work with the other iLife applications—iMovie, iDVD, iPhoto, and GarageBand—to add or augment the specialties of those applications with your iTunes library of songs.

Use iTunes with iMovie

iTunes and iMovie are natural companions—after all, what's a movie without a good soundtrack? Using the iMovie interface, you can dig directly into your iTunes Library to add songs to the videos that you edit. This includes songs that you import from CD, translate from other formats, and even songs that you've bought from the iTunes Music Store.

Here's how to add songs from iTunes to your video presentation in iMovie:

1. In iMovie, decide where you're going to want the song to begin and place the playhead at that point in your edited video.

2. Choose the Audio button in the effects panel. (It's on the right side of the window.)

3. At the top of that pane, choose iTunes Library from the menu. (You can also choose a particular iTunes playlist if you prefer.)

4. Now, select a song. You can click the Play button to hear that song played if you're still trying to decide. (The volume control underneath the playback window can be used to change the volume as you're listening to songs. Click the Play button again to stop playback.)

5. When you find the song you like, click the Place at Playhead button. That puts the song on the lower audio track in the Timeline view of your view. (Even if you were previously in the Clip Viewer, you'll be switched to the Timeline view.)

Now you can edit the audio in all the ways that iMovie allows, including trimming it back to fit your video and editing the volume (click the Edit Volume option) to create fade in and fade out effects. Your song will now be matched with the edited video in whatever your final output is, whether you export the video to QuickTime or send it back to your camcorder for playback on television or for recording to DVD. Likewise, if you move that video on to iDVD to create a movie DVD, your soundtrack, courtesy of iTunes, goes along for the ride.

Use iTunes with iDVD

iDVD is software that enables you to take clips or entire videos that you've created in iMovie and burn them to a movie DVD that can be played back in a typical DVD home player. And, as you've seen, the soundtracks that you add to your iMovie using iTunes goes along for the ride when you move your clips to iDVD.

So what's the direct connection in iDVD? If you've watched commercial DVDs, you know that the menus often have their own audio that plays while you're moving through selections taking a look at the DVD's options and menus. Well, you can do that in iDVD, by adding songs out of your iTunes library to the menu screens that you create in iDVD. Here's how:

1. In iDVD, make sure the customize drawer is open (click the Customize button if it's not).

2. At the top of the Customize drawer, click the Media button.

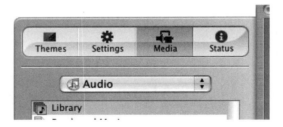

3. From the menu, choose Audio.

4. Now you can see your iTunes Library. There are three things you can do here:

   ■ Select a song and click the Play button to preview it.

■ If you're editing a regular DVD menu, drag a song from the iTunes list to the menu window. Drop it anywhere in the window and it's added as the background song for that menu. (You can also click the Apply button if you don't want to drag the song.)

■ If you're editing a slideshow (click the SlideShow button to add a slideshow to your DVD interface), you can drag a song title to the Audio "well" (which is sort of a reversed button) that appears below the image thumbnails. That sets the song that's used as background music for the slideshow. (When you drop the song, an icon for it appears in that well.)

NOTE   *The Slide Duration option can be set to Fit to Audio. This makes it so that your slideshow lasts the same amount of time as your song.*

C

So what if you have a long DVD slideshow and want more than one song? First, think carefully about whether people really want to sit through that long of a slideshow! If they do, you have two options. First, you can edit the slideshow in iMovie and make it as long as you want (and add as many songs as you want, chopping them up as you please). Second, you can edit together a song file that has more than one song back to back—do that using a song editor, as described in Chapter 9.

Use iTunes with iPhoto

You've seen iMovie and iDVD—what can iTunes add to iPhoto? Actually, it's just a little more of the same that you saw in iDVD—you can use iPhoto to choose the background music for your slideshow in iPhoto. Here's how:

1. In iPhoto, choose a photo album that you want to use for your slideshow.

2. Click the SlideShow button to get to the SlideShow options.

3. In the Slideshow dialog box that appears, click the Music tab.

4. Now, from the Source menu, choose iTunes Library.

5. Next, pick a song and click the Play button. The Slideshow will begin playing with that song as background.

Actually, that's not the only way you can do it. If you'd like multiple songs to play for this slideshow, you can simply select one of your iTunes playlists from the menu and, without choosing a song, click Play. Now, songs from the entire playlist will play as long as you have images for iPhoto to display.

 *Like the choices you've made? Click the SlideShow button again to see those options and, with all the settings the way you want them, click the Save Settings button in the Slideshow dialog box. Now, the next time you play your slideshow (by clicking the Play button in the Slideshow dialog box), it will play with the same music and other setting choices you made and saved.*

Use iTunes with GarageBand

Well, it seems obvious that GarageBand would be a natural fit for working together with iTunes. Once you've put a song together, GarageBand enables you to export that song to a playlist in iTunes. Now you can play it back whenever you want or use it elsewhere in your iLife work—as a soundtrack in iMovie, or for your slideshows in iDVD or iPhoto.

To export a song from GarageBand to iTunes, first create the song. (That could take a while.) When you're ready to send it to iTunes, choose File | Export to iTunes. You'll see GarageBand create a *mixdown,* which means it's turning the song into a single song file.

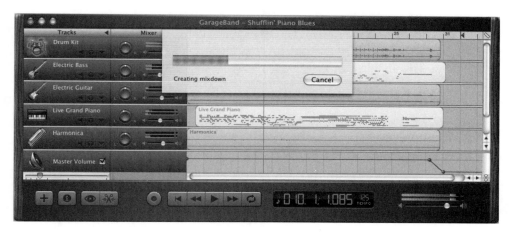

When it's done, the song shows up in a new playlist in iTunes, ready to do your bidding in iTunes and elsewhere. It'll even have your name on it!

▲	Song Name	Time	Artist	Album	Ge
1	☑ Shufflin' Piano Blues	0:57	Todd Stauffer	Todd Stauffer's Album	

Index

INTERNATIONAL CONTACT INFORMATION

AUSTRALIA
McGraw-Hill Book Company
Australia Pty. Ltd.
TEL +61-2-9900-1800
FAX +61-2-9878-8881
http://www.mcgraw-hill.com.au
books-it_sydney@mcgraw-hill.com

CANADA
McGraw-Hill Ryerson Ltd.
TEL +905-430-5000
FAX +905-430-5020
http://www.mcgraw-hill.ca

GREECE, MIDDLE EAST, & AFRICA
(Excluding South Africa)
McGraw-Hill Hellas
TEL +30-210-6560-990
TEL +30-210-6560-993
TEL +30-210-6560-994
FAX +30-210-6545-525

MEXICO (Also serving Latin America)
McGraw-Hill Interamericana Editores
S.A. de C.V.
TEL +525-1500-5108
FAX +525-117-1589
http://www.mcgraw-hill.com.mx
carlos_ruiz@mcgraw-hill.com

SINGAPORE (Serving Asia)
McGraw-Hill Book Company
TEL +65-6863-1580
FAX +65-6862-3354
http://www.mcgraw-hill.com.sg
mghasia@mcgraw-hill.com

SOUTH AFRICA
McGraw-Hill South Africa
TEL +27-11-622-7512
FAX +27-11-622-9045
robyn_swanepoel@mcgraw-hill.com

SPAIN
McGraw-Hill/
Interamericana de España, S.A.U.
TEL +34-91-180-3000
FAX +34-91-372-8513
http://www.mcgraw-hill.es
professional@mcgraw-hill.es

UNITED KINGDOM, NORTHERN,
EASTERN, & CENTRAL EUROPE
McGraw-Hill Education Europe
TEL +44-1-628-502500
FAX +44-1-628-770224
http://www.mcgraw-hill.co.uk
emea_queries@mcgraw-hill.com

ALL OTHER INQUIRIES Contact:
McGraw-Hill/Osborne
TEL +1-510-420-7700
FAX +1-510-420-7703
http://www.osborne.com
omg_international@mcgraw-hill.com

Sound Off!

Visit us at **www.osborne.com/bookregistration** and let us know what you thought of this book. While you're online you'll have the opportunity to register for newsletters and special offers from McGraw-Hill/Osborne.

We want to hear from you!

Sneak Peek

Visit us today at **www.betabooks.com** and see what's coming from McGraw-Hill/Osborne tomorrow!

Based on the successful software paradigm, Bet@Books™ allows computing professionals to view partial and sometimes complete text versions of selected titles online. Bet@Books™ viewing is free, invites comments and feedback, and allows you to "test drive" books in progress on the subjects that interest you the most.

Know How

**How to Do Everything
with Your Digital Camera**
Third Edition
ISBN: 0-07-223081-9

**How to Do Everything
with Photoshop Elements 2**
ISBN: 0-07-222638-2

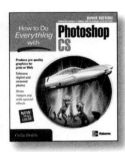

**How to Do Everything
with Photoshop CS**
ISBN: 0-07-223143-2
4-color

**How to Do Everything
with Your Sony CLIÉ**
Second Edition
ISBN: 0-07-223074-6

**How to Do Everything
with Macromedia
Contribute**
0-07-222892-X

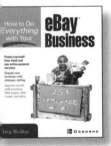

**How to Do Everything
with Your eBay Business**
0-07-222948-9

**How to Do Everything
with Illustrator CS**
ISBN: 0-07-223092-4
4-color

**How to Do Everything
with Your iPod**
ISBN: 0-07-222700-1

**How to Do Everything
with Your iMac,**
Third Edition
ISBN: 0-07-213172-1

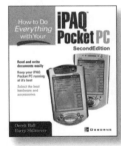

**How to Do Everything
with Your iPAQ Pocket PC**
Second Edition
ISBN: 0-07-222950-0

ORNE

McGraw Osbo

www.osborne

Brilliance

Enlightened answers for your electronics, computers, and applications